About this Book

A Book of Troth is the most comprehensive guide to the elder Teutonic folk-way ever to be produced. With roots in the ancient religion of the Teutonic peoples of Northern Europe, Scandinavia and Iceland, the Troth offers to modern man a set of guidelines for living according to loyalty, brotherhood and personal experience of the gods.

As a basic text, *A Book of Troth* offers an outline of knowledge and experience which the student can use for further exploration of this still-living religion. One part consists of basic theories and lore, another of ritual workings and practices, and the third an outline of the Ring of Troth, the official organization of members of the Troth.

Anyone wishing to explore the mysterious roots of the Teutonic folk religion will find a mine of information and guidance in *A Book of Troth*. Although hidden and repressed for centuries, these ancient principles and practices still ring true for initiate and novice alike.

"The Troth is a way of doing, not of believing. Therefore the deeds of a man or woman are much more important to whether or not they are held to be true than is some doctrine or faith they might believe or defend. Only "work" (that is, actions) will make one's word true. Therefore, work in the Troth and become that which you already are!"

—Edred Thorsson

About the Author

Edred Thorsson, who is a recognized *godhi* or priest in two Ásatrú, or Odinist, religious groups, now holds the offices of the Drighten of the Troth and the Warden of the Lore in the Ring of Troth. For over fifteen years he has dedicated himself to the study and practice of the path of Woden in all its various forms. For several years he led a kindred of the Ásatrú Free Assembly. Edred holds a Ph.D. in Germanic Religious and Magical Studies and has been Yrmin-Drighten of the Rune-Gild since 1980.

To Write to the Author

We cannot guarantee that every letter written to the author can be answered, but all will be forwarded. Both the author and the publisher appreciate hearing from readers, learning of your enjoyment and benefit from this book. Llewellyn also publishes a bi-monthly news magazine with news and reviews of practical esoteric studies and articles helpful to the student, and some readers' questions and comments to the author may be answered through this magazine's columns if permission to do so is included in the original letter. The author sometimes participates in seminars and workshops, and dates and places are announced in *The Llewellyn New Times*. To write to the author, or to ask a question, write to:

Edred Thorsson
c/o THE LLEWELLYN NEW TIMES
P.O. Box 64383-777, St. Paul, MN 55164-0383, U.S.A.
Please enclose a self-addressed, stamped envelope for reply, or $1.00 to cover costs.

Llewellyn's Teutonic Magick Series

Teutonic magick is as vast as the northern sky and as deep as the shrouded northern mists.

Many of the most powerful forms of magick in the West were developed to an early perfection by Teutonic magicians: Albertus Magnus, Agrippa, Paracelsus. Some, such as Faustus, were elevated to legends.

Teutonic magick is multifaceted and it has its own innate traditions—those of the ancient Germanic peoples (Anglo-Saxons, Germans, Dutch, Scandinavians). In addition it has incorporated the general Western Tradition, which the Teutonic magicians received from southern Europe in the Middle Ages and proceeded to develop with characteristic scientific zeal.

The world of Teutonic Magick is full of truly secret, and some sinister, corners as well. Many of these, like so much else that we believe to be sinister, are thus characterized simply because they are unknown and perhaps also misunderstood. There are whole realms of Teutonic magick that have largely been kept secret until the latter part of this century.

Llewellyn's Teutonic Magick Series is the first to explore this world in a systematic and authoritative way. It will reveal the secrets of German rune magic, the obscure mysteries of Gothic Kabbalah, the magic of Faustus, and the deepest mysteries of the German occult orders such as the Rosicrucians, the Illuminati, the Fraternitas Saturni, and the dreaded FOGC-Lodge.

The path of Teutonic magick is focused on the expansion of consciousness through a will to power and knowledge—the way opened for the Teutonic magician by the archetype Woden and followed by Faustus and most modern magicians.

Other Books by Edred Thorsson:

Forthcoming:

Llewellyn's Teutonic Magick Series

A BOOK OF TROTH

by

Edred Thorsson

Ódhinsgodhi
Yrmin-Drighten

1992
Llewellyn Publications
St. Paul, Minnesota, U.S.A., 55164-0383

Cover Painting: N. Taylor Blanchard
Cover Design: Christopher Wells

First Edition
Second Printing, 1992

Library of Congress Cataloging-in-Publications Data
Thorsson, Edred,
  A Book of Troth / by Edred Thorsson.
  p. cm— (Llewellyn's Teutonic magick series)
  Includes bibliographical references.
  ISBN 0-87542-777-4
  1. Teutonic tribes—Religion. I. Title. II. Series.
BL860.T52   1989
299—dc20   89-38817
                                                   CIP

Llewellyn Publications
A Division of Llewellyn Worldwide, Ltd.
P.O. Box 64383, St. Paul, MN 55164-0383

thjódhunni

Acknowledgments

I would like to thank my many academic mentors, without whose help this synthesis could not have been reached. At the same time, I would also like to thank my wife, Nancy, for having put up with my indulgences for many years. I also gladly acknowledge the help given to me by my principal advisors and associates, Mitchell Edwin Wade (Ódhinsgodhi), James Allen Chisholm (steersman), David Bragwin James, Robert Zoller, and John Yeowell, Director of the Odinic Rite. Thanks also to Marnie Anderson, Alice Rhoades, Stephen A. McNallen, Thorsteinn Thorarinsson, and many other true men and women who helped make the way to the gods and goddesses clear.

Contents

Preface

This is a book ten years in the making. When I first joined the Ásatrú Free Assembly in the late 1970s, I trusted that it would carry forth the efforts in the revival of our old and timeless folk ways. But circumstances conspired to bring the AFA to an untimely end. It was at the point of the demise of this organization that it became clear to me that the thousands of pages of notes, rituals, articles, and so on that I had produced while running a local kindred for several years finally had to find expression in *A Book of Troth*. Only in this way could that storehouse of information be preserved in the actual practice of good folk and true.

A Book of Troth is not a "holy book" or a "bible" in the usual sense. This concept is totally foreign to our true ways. But it is certainly the most traditionally based and well-informed general guide to the practice of the elder Germanic folk way ever to be produced. As an outline of the Troth it is as complete a guide as anyone would need use to practice their ancestral faith in private.

The Troth is a way of doing, a way of action, and not so much a way of believing or a way of doctrine. Although the system is capable of philosophical sophistication far beyond that of superstitious Middle Eastern cults such as Judaism, Christianity, or Islam, it is first and foremost a code of behavior and a set of actions to be carried out faithfully.

In this way, it has sometimes been compared to the Shinto religion of Japan. When we look to Japan these days, we may remark on many things that set it apart from our own society. But one thing remains valid about the Japanese: they have mastered the 20th century without ever having to leave their ancestral past. That is, they have hit upon a certain secret of how to adapt to radically new situations without having to sell their souls to exotic and foreign gods. The secret is in the way of their ancestral gods and god-desses—the timeless inner heart of the folk that when built on authentic principles lends an undying strength to all endeavors. This is a way of doing, much more than a "faith" in certain dogmas. The Troth seeks the same for our folk.

A Book of Troth is the official, basic document of the organization known simply as "The Ring of Troth." More information on the structure of this organization can be found in part three of this book.

The method used to write this volume is very similar to that which I used in writing my three rune books. It is a synthesis of the most recent and sophisticated academic scholarship into which I was "initiated," through graduate studies programs in Germanic philology from 1976 to 1984, and the practical ritual work and teaching cycles carried out within the Austin Kindred of the AFA from about 1978 to 1983. The science was quickened by the work and the work was informed by the science. Through this delicate methodology a result is gained which, I hope, will speak to the heart as well as to the mind; and it will bring a result that both the strict scientist and the folkish mystic can embrace. For the Troth there has always been room for all—so it was, so it is, and so it shall be!

Introduction

A Book of Troth consists of three parts: one of basic theories and lore, another of basic practices and ritual workings, and a third which contains an outline of the structure of the Ring of Troth. What is essential to keep in mind when reading and studying the contents of this book is that it is a basic text. It does not purport to be complete, but rather is supposed to be fundamental. From information and practices imparted through this book anyone can begin to be true and to act in a true way.

All those who are truly serious about the Troth as defined in this book will probably want to become sworn members of the Troth, the address of which can be found on the acknowledgments page of this volume. However, even if you do not choose to do this, all those who adhere to the basic tenets of this book, and who in some way observe the Great Blessings of the Year, are still considered true to the olden way.

The first part of this book consists of 23 short chapters on important topics within the Troth. Any one of them could be the subject for one or more whole books. What I have tried to convey is a basic approach, with a minimum of speculation to each of these topics. Fortunately, within our wide-ranging, pluralistic theology there is room for many divergent views. However, one difficulty arising from this generally happy situation is that many times no single definitive answer can be given to fundamental questions, for many things may be true. Where well-founded variants in viewpoint are known, they will be mentioned.

The heart of this work is to be found in its second part. The Troth is a way of doing, not of believing. Therefore the deeds of a man or woman are much more important to whether or not they are held to be true than is some doctrine or article of faith that they might believe or defend. Much of this "true work" is done in one's everyday life, to be sure. But what is most essential, and minimal, from a religious point of view is that the true man or woman take part in the four Greatest Blessings of the Year—Winter Nights, Yule, Easter and Midsummer.

All in all, it is a mainstay of the Troth that doing should come before believing. Only "work" (that is, actions) will make one's word true. Therefore, work in the Troth and become that which you already are. The instructions given in this book will enable the reader to begin tonight to practice the ancestral Troth. The true man or woman will usually begin to practice privately and alone. As the Troth grows within, however, most will want to associate and have fellowship with other true men and women. For this purpose the official organizational aspects of the Ring of Troth exist.

In the last part of this book there is an outline of the structure and nature of the Troth as an organization and of its Eldership. Although we expect that some will want to continue to practice truly in private and in small groups (kindreds) apart from the main branch of the Troth, most would greatly benefit—intellectually, socially, and spiritually—from association with the Ring of Troth. Also in this third part there is a fairly detailed outline of the training that must be undergone and qualifications that must be met before one can be named as Elder in the Ring of Troth.

A Book of Troth is dedicated to the folk (*thjódhunni*) that it may kindle in each heart a flame, and so that when it comes together with other flames to be hallowed on some Mother Night the whole of the folk may be taken up in a great enlightenment. In that night we will see the beginning of a new world, in which that which was will be again. Then the old ones will return, not just to rule in quiet corners unseen but to reign supreme again over all the lands of all their children. Once the world was true—make it so again.

Guide to Pronunciation of Old Norse Words

Usually the consonants *b, d, f, k, l,* and *v* are as in modern English.

á	as in *father*
a	as in *artistic*
é	as *ay* in *bay*
e	as in *men*
í	as *ee* in *feet*
i	as in *it*
ó	as in *omit*
o	as in *ore*
ö	as in *not*
ø	same as o
ú	as in *rule*
u	as in *put*
ǽ	as *ai* in *hair*
œ̂	as *u* in *slur*
ŷ	as in German *Tur—ee* with rounded lips
y	as in German *Hutte—i* with rounded lips
au	as *ou* in *house*
ei	as *i* in *ice*
ey	same as ei
g	always hard as in *go*
ng	always as in *long*—never as in *finger*
h	same as English except before consonants, then as *wh* in *where*
j	as English *y* in *year*
p	as in English, except before *t*; then this *pt* cluster is pronounced *ft*

r	trilled *r*
s	voiceless as in *sing*, except after *r*; then as *sh*
th	in initial position voiceless as in *thin*
dh	in medial or final position voiced *th* as in *then*
ll	pronounced *dl* after long vowels and diphthongs
rl	pronounced *dl*
rn	pronounced *dn*
nn	pronounced *dn* after long vowels and diphthongs

Part I
Being True

1

Troth

What is "troth"? It does seem nowadays to be a curious word, rather archaic sounding, perhaps a bit legalistic. But it is in the essence of this word that the true path can be found by those who seek to follow the old way of the North. This is a partial answer to the question, and it is hoped that this will crystallize the idea for those who might find themselves within its parameters, as well as show the true essence of this, the troth of our forebears.

The conditions in which we now find ourselves—in a Christian cult of guilt, hypocrisy, and alienation, are mainly a result of the lack of information about the true nature of the timeless ways of our folk. Christianity, in all its various shapes and forms, consumes a large number of people, and the rationalist/materialist cult grabs up most of the leftovers. This latter group tends to abhor the outer trappings of the Christian cults, while eagerly pursuing its own methodology and many of its aims. This is largely due to its tendency to swallow dogmatic, authoritarian approaches left over from the nineteenth century. It is astounding that some schools of thought trying to revive our ways still believe in the interpretation of our mythology formulated by "scientists" who considered our (their!) ancestors silly savages who merely "worshipped" trees and rocks!

The word "troth" may now only be known from the formula of some ancient marriage vows—"I plight my troth in thee," which simply means: "I place my trust, loyalty, or faith, in you." Another form of the same root word is found in the adjective "true," as in one who is true (loyal) to a cause or to a principle. The Troth is a religious path derived directly from our ancestors. There is no need to resort to exotic terminologies from Hebrew, Greek, Latin, Sanskrit, or even from Old Norse for that matter. We can therefore happily use English and not exotic tongues when speaking of our religious concepts. To be forced to use foreign tongues (even those to which we are greatly indebted, such as Icelandic) would give a lie to all for which we stand: the fundamental faith of our forebears. When we say the *Troth*, we are simply saying the *religion* of the people speaking the language in which the term is expressed. In this instance it is the Germanic English tongue. When we say that a man or woman is "true," we mean to say that he or she is loyal (to the ways of his or her ancestors). That it seems to imply that those who are not "true" in this way are somehow not as authentic as those who are so called may also indicate something!

In order to gain a deeper understanding of what "troth" means, we can look at the Icelandic term *ásatrú*. The word is a compound of *ása-*, "of the gods (æsir)," and *-trú*, usually translated as "faith." But this can be misleading. *Tru* is derived from the same root (*deru-*) that gave rise to "troth," "truth," "trust," and "true" in English. The root word *deru-* really has to do with something firm, solid, and steadfast. The fact that the word "tree" also comes from this word is significant as well. Therefore it is clear that originally the term had more of the connotations of our "true" (loyal), "trusting," and "troth" than with the connotations of "faith" or "belief."

Belief is the acceptance through an external authority that a given thing is true, and perhaps that some form of "salvation" is dependent on this belief. Troth is based on experience. One trusts that the sun will come up tomorrow because this recurring phenomenon has been experienced in the past. The things that one is commanded to believe in Christianity, Judaism, Islam, Marxism, etc., are precisely those things one cannot experience, or those things known only to pastors, popes, rabbis, imams, commissars, etc. "To trust" therefore is to gain personal experience of the truth of a thing. The term *ásatrú* therefore most literally means "gaining experience of the ancestral sovereign gods." To see the new dawn one must look toward the East in the morning; to see the gods one must look to them in times of great blessing.

The ways of true men and women are many. The Ring of Troth promotes a multiplicity of approaches to the gods and goddesses, for the realities of these beings are many and have many true levels.

The essence of the Troth, however, remains the seeking of this personal experience (leading to troth) in and of the gods in a way similar to the way one can experience the sunrise. The sun and the phenomenon of her rising are physical manifestations; the gods are more complex. To know the gods and goddesses one must seek them out in all the worlds. It is the task of all who would follow the old way of the North to seek the truth of personal experience at its source. This is always a positive power, welling up from within and growing in freedom. Once attained, these internal powers render impotent any oppression from external sources. An invincible holy fortress is built which may undergo infinite evolution without ever being "destroyed." This, the rune of Ragnarök, lying within the last stave, has until now escaped many who would follow the Troth.

2

The Way

The Troth is based on what one does, or what one experiences. It is not based on external authority from any source. The Troth grows from within the folk, and from within the individual. This does not mean, however, that it is totally subjective or without authentic standards—far from it. But the way we use to arrive at what is true is somewhat more complicated than just believing what a TV preacher says, or deriving what little meaning can be derived from the historicized mythology of some vanished race.

Members of the Troth arrive at what is true through a three-fold method of inquiry and observation. The method stands on three leys:

1) the historical tradition
2) observation of the world
3) personal experience

All three are taken into account on all questions.

The historical tradition includes all the mythological and historical material we have concerning the ancient Teutonic and Indo-European peoples. No "Teutonic bible" exists. The *Poetic* and *Prose Eddas* are the most complete guidebooks to the shape of the elder mythology, and are

5

our best primary evidence in this realm, but they are by no means considered "the word of the gods."

When looking at the historical tradition, another three-fold process is used:

1) rational/scientific
2) transpersonal psychological
3) personal/subjective

These three approaches are hierarchized in order of primacy, with the rational laying the foundations, the transpersonal psychological expanding on what is known from the rational, and the subjective deepening and personalizing the other two.

It is also imperative to realize that there are levels of importance to the historical evidence. Maximum weight is given to the oldest and most direct sources of the Teutonic tradition itself. Less important are the indirect sources, i.e. accounts about the ancestors written by outsiders (Romans, Greeks, etc.). Later interpretive concoctions that do not ring true to these ancient sources should be taken with a block of salt.

The interpretation and employment of these sources is indeed a complicated matter. It is in this area, and in the technical aspects of carrying out the Great Blessings of the Troth, that the priesthood is most necessary.

Once a traditional basis has been established on a question, environmental observation becomes very important. This is something that goes beyond what might be considered "observation of nature" today. We should look in an objective way at how the world revolves around a given question. We would ask: "What does the natural environment have to say?" and "What does the social environment have to say?" The objective environment can have the effect of altering or evolving the tenets of tradition. But in order for it to do so, it must be well founded and beneficial.

Finally, personal and subjective factors are to be considered. These are very tricky. If you have determined through the application of the first two factors that the answer to a given question is one thing, but based on your own subjective feelings and reflections you lean in an opposite direction, then you should by all means follow your heart. But you should keep such things to yourself, and not then try to force this subjective conclusion on other true folk. After all, it is you who are out of step with the tradition, and the burden of proof is on you. Also, it makes a large difference as to the nature and power of the Self being observed. Elders may have to do a great deal of soul-searching on certain matters, but because of their training, the souls they are searching through are mighty indeed, and so their conclusions may be more valid than those of untrained or unschooled souls.

Of course, in practical terms, these all represent matters of refinement rather than the essentials of the Troth, which remain firmly rooted in the simplicity of the Great Blessings.

For the sake of demonstration, let us ask a question which is of some importance to the re-establishment of the Troth: "Should the Troth have a full-time professional priesthood?" Factor 1): All historical evidence points to there having been a full-time priesthood in the most ancient times, and for this priest-class to have been involved in matters of state as well as of religion. This was stronger in the most ancient times, while in Viking Age Iceland the role of statesman was largely the most important one for a "priest." But it is undeniable that the post that the *godhi* held was originally a *sacral* one. Factor 2): Today most religions functioning in European and North American culture have professional priesthoods of one kind or another. (This despite the fact that professionalism was originally not a part of primitive Christianity.) The Troth demands that its priesthood be trained, educated and committed in mind as well as heart. 3): Many in Ásatrú/Odinism today wish that there would be no professional priests in the Troth. In this they may be following noble instincts that perhaps go back to their longing for a non-hypocritical Christian cult—in which a professional priesthood would be quite impossible. Others in the Troth wish to be able to devote themselves full-time to the re-establishment of the religion of their ancestors—or wish to be able to have personal access to someone who has undertaken this course in life.

The conclusion seems to be that a professional priesthood is warranted according to tradition and necessity, and that those who oppose it should search their souls for the roots of this feeling.

3

The Elder History

It is clear that in the Troth we are not merely reduced to reviving dead forms. The true Troth never died within us; we only became, for a time, unaware of its timeless presence. Therefore, we never get ourselves in the pointlessly anachronistic position of saying: "In days of yore the ancestors did things in this way or that, and therefore we must imitate their actions in order to be true." It is the time-less spirit and quality of their deeds that is worth imitating, not necessarily the outer forms. It is for this reason that meticulous historical reconstructions and historical studies, although avidly pursued by many Elders, are in general not of primary importance to the true man or true woman of today. Their Troth is proven in their true deeds and doings and by the ways in which they live and work, not in the amount of lore and eldrich wisdom they have gathered in their heads.

However, one of the central problems confronting the modern Troth is the level of ignorance and misinforma-tion—sometimes even disinformation—among its own folk surrounding its origins and heritage. A historical digression to place what is written here in some context is needed.

The Troth is the timeless and manifold religious path

of the Germanic, or Teutonic, peoples. Why and how it is timeless and manifold will be made clear in later chapters. But just what is meant by Teutonic? This word sometimes carries with it some negative connotations, which are more reflective of the growing negative self-image of the Teutonic peoples than of anything present in the objective world.

Let us start with the fact that most of the people now reading these words are primarily of Teutonic ethnic stock, descended from persons of English (Anglo-Saxon), German (as well as Austrian and Swiss), Norwegian, Danish, Swedish, Dutch, or Icelandic nationality. Most of the others, whether of Irish, Scots, French, Italian, Spanish, Polish, or Czech background, will probably have significant amounts of Teutonic blood in their veins. Each of these national groups have been at one time or another, in one way or another, heavily Teutonicized, either ethnically or ethically. That is, their cultural ideals and values have been transformed into essentially Teutonic ones. With the advent of the English language (an essentially Teutonic tongue) as the leading language of the world, and the rise of the Teutonic ideal—perverted as it might have become over time—of political governance by the will of the governed, we have seen the virtual Teutonization of the whole world in the last two centuries.

Beginning about 1000 B.C.E. a group of Indo-European folk living in the area of what is now southern Scandinavia and northern Germany began to set themselves apart from the surrounding Indo-European and non-Indo-European peoples in linguistic, cultural, and religious ways. The founding cultural and ethnic stock from which the Teutonic peoples developed had probably come from somewhere in the East, from the regions around the Caspian Sea, or from the southern Russian steppe area. This migration began about 4000 B.C.E. and lasted to perhaps 1000 B.C.E.

This was part of the great Indo-European migrations which eventually colonized Asia Minor, Iran, India, Greece, Italy, and all of Europe.

These Indo-European peoples share a common linguistic, cultural, and religious heritage; but as they became more and more distant from one another in time and space they developed even more diverse characteristics in their languages, cultures, and religions. However, each continues to share a common primeval bond. When the process of differentiation had reached a certain stage in northern Europe, the Teutonic peoples could be said to have come into being.

It is always the religion of a people that preserves the most ancient ways of that folk. So in the greater troth of the Teutonic peoples we see most clearly the traces of the ancient Indo-European heritage. The essence of the troth was, and is, the maintenance of a bond of loyalty between the gods and goddesses, who provide the gifts of knowledge, wisdom, valor, strength, plenty, and pleasure, and humankind, who provide for the continuance of the gods and goddesses. All are dedicated to the common goal of maintaining, and where possible widening, the sphere of godly consciousness throughout the worlds. This troth was for centuries a continuously and naturally evolving thing, at once defining and being defined by the culture of which it was an organic part. Had there not been outside interference, this process would have continued and we would probably still honor the great gods and goddesses of our ancestors—much as the Hindus of India still honor their ancestral divinities.

This interference in our national self-determination came in the form of a cult from the East called Christianity. It is amusing to hear its adherents wail in horror as "our culture" is invaded by "Eastern cults," as Christianity itself is one of those cults. That they know this on some level is probably responsible for the intensity of their hysteria. To compound the irony, many of the "cults" imported from India may indeed be more "Western"; that is, they may be more closely tied to our own indigenous religious heritage than is Christianity. After all, the Vedas and Eddas share a common origin; the Torah and its appendices (the New Testament, the Koran, etc.) may as well have come from different planets.

But by various methods—heretical camouflage, military force, cabal, or socio-economic coercion—Christianity marched not only over the other peoples of Europe—Greek, Roman, Gaelic, and Brithonic—but eventually also into the Teutonic homeland. Finally, the great hof at Uppsala fell in 1100. The last nation to fall, Germania was the first to throw off the domination of the foreign-controlled church of Rome.

It should be briefly recounted how our folk fell victim to this force. First, it must generally be realized that one of our basic strengths is also our chief "soft spot": the innate toleration of others and an inherent interest in things foreign and exotic. Let it suffice to say that no other folk has so enthusiastically pursued the concept of "human rights," or more enthusiastically traveled over the whole world, as explorers, conquerors, colonizers, and now as tourists. This is without doubt a great source of strength on many levels but its existence and nature must be realized in order for it to be a cultural asset and not a liability. It only becomes a liability when those who are tolerant and who are fascinated by the exotic meet with the forces of intolerance and xenophobia. When the ancient German met a Christian he was probably interested in what the Christian had to say, never thinking that this acquaintance would try to turn the true man into a Christian. The Christian easily took advantage of this situation, because it was always his plan to subvert the true man's life and culture. It is in the very nature and essence of Christianity to do so.

If it were only this question of the tolerant, and sometimes naive, running up against the forces of intolerant cunning, the forces of the elder troth would have probably been able to withstand the Christian cultural invasion. But things were actually more complex.

In order to illustrate four types of these complexities, we will recount the conversions of four groups of Teutonic folk: the Goths, who fell through an attractive Christian heresy; the Franks, who cunningly made an alliance with a foreign power; the Saxons, who were conquered by the Franks and converted by the sword; and the Icelanders, who quietly and ever so slowly succumbed to the socio-economic pressures of the establishment on the European continent.

The Goths were evangelized in the fourth century by a man known as Bishop Wulfila (or Ulfilas), who had been taken captive in the Roman Empire and converted to Christianity. However, the form of Christianity to which he was converted was not Roman Catholicism, but the so-called Arian heresy. This theological variation was in fact more logical, straightforward, and humane than that of orthodoxy. It held that the "father," "son" and "holy ghost" were in truth three entities, that Jesus was an ordinary man who had attained god-like status by means of his will, and that all men were not tainted by the "sin" of Adam and Eve. This, by the way, is in total contrast with orthodox notions which are still officially adhered to by all Western Christian sects, Protestant and Catholic. Orthodoxy holds that the "father," "son," and "holy ghost" are three and one simultaneously, that all people are born with original sin (separated from "God"), and that only the gift (grace) of God (not the will of the individual) can "save" that individual. So the Gothic or Arian church started out in theory as a more logical and humane institution. It was to this form of Christianity that various Teutonic folk—the Ostrogoths, Visigoths, Burgundians, Vandals, etc., originally came. What is most important to realize about this faith, however, is the fact that it was a thoroughly Teutonic church. The Bible was at once translated into Gothic. There is good evidence to show that this was more of the old Gothic troth with an overlay of Christian symbols and mythology than anything else. Nevertheless it was a giant step toward the ruin of the elder troth. The Christian deity had entered the cultural arena in a place of honor.

The Gothic church was, however, anathema to the Roman church and had to be destroyed. The Goths dominated the entire Western Roman Empire from 410 (when the Visigoths sacked Rome) to the end of the Gothic Wars in 553. Against their rule the pope plotted constantly. His natural allies were the Franks, who were the military and cultural rivals of the Goths. The king of the Franks converted to Christianity in 496 under the influence of his Roman Catholic wife. Thus a financial-military alliance was formed between the Catholics and the Franks. From that time forward the Franks became the soldiers of the pope, conquering their Teutonic neighbors and forcing them not only to convert to Roman Catholicism, but also to live in a political state which had no respect for their tribal differences. This politico-religious alliance worked out to the mutual benefit of the Christian church and the forces of the Frankish kings. This is not unlike the situation today in which petty warlords and tin-horn dictators are able to increase their power by making ideological alliances with either Washington or Moscow—alliances which then lead to military and financial aid.

Over the next few centuries the Franks employed a combination of military tactics and subversive "missionary" activity to weaken and destroy the ancient traditions of their Teutonic neighbors. One of the most telling episodes in this period occurred when a mission reached the region of present-day Holland around the year 696. The Christian missionary Willibrord tried to convert the king of the Frisians, Radbod. Just before being baptized, Radbod asked the priest if he would be with his ancestors the great kings of the Frisians when he died. The priest answered that the ancestors would be in Hell, for they had not come to know Christ, while he on the contrary would find himself in Heaven on the right hand of God. Radbod replied that he would rather be in Hell with his great and noble ancestors than in Heaven with a bunch of beggars!

In the reign of the Frankish king Karl "the Great," or Charlemagne, the most direct form of military conquest as a way of converting the folk to Christianity was adopted. From 772 to 804, Karl waged war on the true Saxons. In 782 at Werden the Franks committed an act of genocide on the Saxon nobility—the true athlings—in which 4,500 were executed for refusing to bow down to the law of the Christians. When subversion failed, the Christian forces would always bring more persuasive tools to bear.

When some of the Saxons were formally converted to Christianity, they were coerced into making baptismal vows which read in part:

"Forsakest thou the devils?"
(he responds):"I forsake the devils! And I forsake all devilish sacrifices! And all devilish works!"
(he responds): "And I forsake all the works and words of the devil, and Thunar, and Woden and Saxnote and all those who are their companions."

The Troth uses a ceremony designed to reverse this coerced oath. The cause of our noble ancestors is not lost or forgotten.

Why this is so is made clear in chapter 28.

Once the economic power centers on the European continent were secured, Scandinavia was converted by similar means—conquest and subversion. It was not uncommon for the Christian "missions" to be preceded by gangs of assassins who would set out to kill men and women of knowledge in the land, so that when the Christian forces arrived they would meet with less organized intellectual resistance.

In the so-called "Viking Age" the Christians of Europe were sometimes forbidden to trade with the heathen Northmen until they were "prime-signed." This meant that although they had not yet been baptized, they were preparing for this act. The final outcome of this kind of policy was the economic strangulation of the Northland. This was sharply felt in Iceland, a land with few natural resources and thus very much dependent on trade; economic factors more than anything else therefore led to the legislative adoption of Christianity by the Icelanders in the year 1000. Lest anyone think this was done sincerely, it must be pointed out that even after the "conversion" the practice of the troth continued to be allowed "in private."

For us today, what is essential to know, and what is essential to remember, is that our ancestors were forced in one way or another, against their wills, to convert to a foreign, Eastern cult. Christianity is not the true faith of our land or of our folk. In this age of acute spiritual crisis, it seems the true seeker has but two legitimate choices: to cling to the sinking wreckage of Christianity, the faith which was foisted on us several centuries ago, or to return to our ancestral faith. In returning to the troth, we revive something that has already worked, something proven for many centuries. In rejecting the Christian path, we throw off something that never worked. The very fact that you are reading these words proves the truth of them.

4

Newer History

It may come as a shock to many, but in northern Europe Christianity never really took hold. The conversion of the northern lands was characterized by the most hypocritical and deceitful methods of which Christianity was capable, and the process was undertaken with the least vital of Christian forces. After the North had been nominally converted, it was left more to itself than was any other part of the Christian empire. The result was a rather anemic form of Christianity; and in this way the seeds of Christianity's ultimate downfall in this area were laid. If viewed objectively, it is plain that the northern European countries and their colonies (America, Australia, South Africa, etc.) are Christian in name and sentiment only. We are only awaiting the conscious realization of this and the return of our heritage.

The period between the "conversion" of a people and the return to their spiritual roots is called the period of "mixed faith," or of "blended troth." This is a general principle, not one peculiar to the Teutonic peoples. What makes it particularly obvious in our case is that we were the last to convert (and were converted in the worst ways), and among the first to begin to throw off the yoke of the cross.

A Book of Troth

In the Latinate world the first resurgence of the old religion is characterized by the name Renaissance—"rebirth." This was a great, but in many ways immature, revolutionary return to the values of the classical, pre-Christian world of philosophy and science. What was being reborn in this "rebirth" was the essence of the pagan world. The religious revival, although in certain instances present, was weak. The seeds of blended troth also remained in the Celtic countries of Ireland, Scotland, and Wales.

Throughout the Teutonic world, the period of mixed faith took different yet remarkably similar paths. In England, Germany, and Scandinavia, the cultural life of the courts of the athlings and aristocrats remained a bastion of true values; in the countryside the folk maintained customs inherited from the days of yore.

In Scandinavia, especially in the more remote parts of Norway and Sweden, and in Iceland, fairly open displays of paganism were tolerated. Babies which the parents could not afford to feed, or that were in some way deformed, were exposed (often in churchyards!), and private, heathen sacrifices were held. As for the "forces" of the church, they were quite often the very agents most avidly preserving, if sometimes in covert ways, the heathen traditions. In Iceland the priests enthusiastically collected heathen lore and in some instances wrote it down for the first time, thus preserving it for our use today. The Icelandic scribes would usually record the heathen lore faithfully, and then perhaps comment on it by saying: "We don't believe this anymore." But what was important is that they faithfully recorded this tradition without editing or destroying it.

The ways in which religions are mixed are very important to observe. If we are to "unmix" them, then similar paths might be followed by some groups of individuals. In religion itself, the evidence of faith-mixing is rampant. Many Catholic saints are really nothing more than pagan gods and goddesses in Christian garb. This, coupled with the Catholic "cult of the saints," allowed paganism to continue under the aegis of the church. Examples of this are St. Martin and St. Michael, both understood as Thunar (or Thórr) in the North, or St. Oswald, who is apparently Woden canonized. The name Oswald even means "the power of a god" in Old English. Not only were true legends "Christianized," but so too were rituals and temples. When Augustine was having trouble converting the English in the seventh century A.D., he wrote to Pope Gregory asking what to do. The people continued going to the site of their pagan temples, even though they had been burned to the ground by the forces of the god of love. The pope's advice represents a classic statement of Christian methods. He told Augustine to build a church on the site of the old pagan temple, where he would then have the folk "where he wanted them." This is a physical example of what was also done with festivals and religious holy-days.

The name of the holiday known as Easter is directly derived from the name of the Teutonic goddess of the spring, Eostre, also known as Ostara in Germany. The name of her festival was so strong and so deeply ingrained in the souls of the folk that the forces of Christianity could not remove it, and so it remains today. In Germany the Christmas season is known as *Weihnachten*, which literally means "the holy (*weih*) nights." This name is full of true connotations. First, the old word *weih* expresses a special form of "the holy," one which contains notions of the terrifying and awesome power of the divinity. Also, the form of the word is plural and refers to the twelve nights of the yule-tide. Finally, the fact that nights and not "days" are used in the expression shows that it is a very old term indeed (see chapter 9). One does not have to listen to many bible-thumpers for long to find out that the lovely "Christmas tree" is really a pagan-heathen custom. Its origins are in the true practice of setting out gifts under a holy evergreen tree in the forest for the ancestral dises and elves who were nearby during the yule-tide. The tree itself would typically be draped with holy signs (perhaps made of pastry or bread), and would be brightly illuminated to attract the attention of the wights. When ecclesiastical authorities gained enough power, they tried to coerce the folk to stop this practice. This only forced the people to bring the tree in out of the forest and to continue the practice indoors. Of course, as time went on, the folk began to forget why they did this. But with the pure wisdom of childhood many youngsters know that it is right and true to leave out some gifts (milk and cookies perhaps) for the jolly ol' elf who comes down the chimney—for aye does a gift always look for gain! (Yes, Virginia, it's true: "Santa Claus" is no Christian!)

Historically one area in which heathenry was not purely maintained was in the area of magic and witchcraft. Because such things were generally condemned outright by the church, the lore was relatively free to be as heathen as it wanted to be. Also, because the church condemned such practices as being "of the devil," much of the old pagan lore began to be considered "diabolical" as well.

It was not only in the realm of "religion" that the effects of the period of mixed faith could be felt. Because the ancestors did not make the strict and artificial (but unfortunately still necessary) distinctions between religion and "politics" in days of yore, and because the troth was really a matter of everyday life and custom (and not just a "Sunday-go-t'-meetin' " affair), features of the political, customary, "literary," and material culture also have much to tell us on the nature of the period of mixed faith.

In the realm of what we would generally call "politics" today, certain concepts of the sacred responsibilities of the king and of the rights of the aristocracy were directly inherited from the ancient Teutonic system. The Teutonic king, although many times seen as the descendant of a god and to have sacral functions, was not an all-powerful despot. He ruled at the will of, and through election by, the aristocracy—the athlings of the tribe. When he was no longer able to fulfill his responsibilities, he was deposed. This is a far cry from, but in some superficial ways related to, the Christian idea of the "divine right" of kings.

Our very law is today based on Teutonic cosmic principles. So-called English "Common Law" was inherited from Anglo-Saxon tribal law. This was law based on what had gone before, that is, it was based on precedent. What has happened before shall happen again—so it is right. This can be said for more than the law! (See chapter 19 to see how this relates to Teutonic concepts of cosmic law.)

If we look back to the political realities of the ancient Teutonic world, we will see that they had much more in common with our "modern" conceptions than will be found, for example, in Middle Eastern notions, or in later Christianized ideas of political order. All were based on superstitious coercion.

During the period of mixed faith, some of the everyday aspects of life came under attack by the forces of Christianity. At some time in the heathen past, the Teutonic peoples had called at least some of their weekdays by the names of some of their most important gods and goddesses. The English best preserved these names: Tues-day (Day of Tiw), Wednes-day (Day of Woden), Thus-day (Day of Thunar), Fri-day (Day of Frigga). The Christians, of course, tried to stamp these names out, but the customary names held on. In Germany, for example, one can see how the Christians were partially successful—what should be *Wodesdag* is called *Mittwoch* ("Mid-week"). This is because the name of Woden, the highest of the gods and All-Father, god of magic, skaldcraft, and death, was totally "tabu-ized." The people were forbidden to utter his name!

Many other essentially heathen customs remained. The countryside in most Teutonic countries is still alive with the old ways. They are, however, misunderstood today, or have been reinterpreted to make things more palatable. Everything from the shape and names of pastries and breads to the forms of decoration painted on the houses and on household items shines with heathenry! There is nothing unique in this; the same can be said for Celtic, Italic, or Slavic regions. But fortunately we have very archaic material in the Teutonic world with which we can compare living folk customs with the older strains of the high religion. The seeds have remained, just waiting for the right amount of water to revivify them.

Many of the so-called "fairy tales" we often read to children, or folk tales, contain the seed forms of ancient folk wisdom. These were preserved by being driven "underground." That is, they were largely ignored by the forces of Christianity because they were considered lowly and of little importance. This is a stream of action that runs parallel to the imbedding of heathen ideals in supposedly Christian tales and customs. Between these two tendencies the soul essence of the lore of our ancestors barely survived, in a quite mangled state. But the preservation of actual mythic texts and the fact that the ancestors left their culture buried in the soil of their lands, later to be dug up by descendants eager to learn of their ancient past, has made the revival of what did not survive a very viable possibility. The web of wyrd has worked to our boon!

With all this to work with, it did not take long, in historical terms, for the Teutonic spirit to begin to make an overt comeback. Since that time the road has been a difficult, if necessary, one.

Logically, if a bit ironically, the first overt effort to begin a Teutonic Renaissance was mounted in Sweden, in the middle of the 1500s. At that time the seat of Swedish

power was Uppsala, where the last great heathen temple
had been destroyed in the year 1100. Some three-and-a-
half centuries after the destruction of the last temple, a
new—if only a spiritual—temple was raised on the spot.
The movement responsible for this revival was known by
the Swedish term *storgoticism*, or Great-Gothicism. The
man most responsible for its formal foundation was again,
quite ironically, the last Catholic archbishop of Uppsala,
Johannes Magnus. He was followed by Johannes Bureus,
who was the tutor of the great Swedish king Gustavus
Adolphus. Bureus became the virtual high priest of a revived
Teutonic religion centered in Uppsala. This revived nationalist religion which came as a part of Sweden's breaking
away from Catholic Europe and becoming part of the
growing Protestant movement, (with its national churches
and the kings as head of both state and church), was also
significant in the redevelopment of the old ways. But for all
its good intentions, Great-Gothicism was a rather confused mixture of old Teutonic ideas and notions adopted
from Judaism and Christianity. What is most significant
about Great-Gothicism is that it had as its major premise
the idea that the right path for a Swede was a Swedish (in
their terms, Gothic) path—and not a universal or international one.

    Johannes Bureus was a scholar as well as a mystic. The
fact that one of the fathers of the self-conscious rebirth of
the elder path was a scholar, and a nationalist, is important, for it was in the academic cradle of German Romantic
nationalism that the firmer foundations of the Teutonic
Renaissance were to be laid. In the late 1700s and early
1800s, there was an international movement called "Ro-
manticism," which involved a sense of inwardness, or
turning in to one's own self for a deeper sense of reality and
truth. This subjectivity was in part a reaction to the objec-
tivist approach of so-called "classicism." When applied to

nations rather than people, this inward-turning results in a keen interest in national traditions and folk ways—in the roots of the folk.

Again among the Swedes, this new spirit broke forth with a special vigor. In the early 1800s there were founded two serious organizations, the Gotiska Forbund and the Manhemsforbund, both of which were dedicated not only to literary pursuits but also to the regeneration of the national spirit based on ancient Teutonic values.

This new spirit was taken up with a deep intellectual enthusiasm by the Germans. They began to see that they too, not just the Greeks and Romans, had great national traditions. Scholars and artists began to turn their attention to their own national heritage. But because so much of the elder tradition had been destroyed over the nearly 1,000 years since the "conversion" had taken place in that part of the world, very refined and sophisticated techniques of investigation had to be developed. The resistance provided the whetstone upon which the sword of Tiw could be sharpened.

The most important exponents of the new Romantic spirit and the Germanic Rebirth were the brothers Grimm, Jacob and Wilhelm. Jacob Grimm was the pioneering father of the academic sciences of comparative religion, mythology, and comparative linguistics (he formulated the basic linguistic law that demonstrates the organic relationship between Teutonic and the other Indo-European languages), and the science of folklore. The brothers Grimm went out into the field and collected their *Märchen* ("fairy tales") as an exercise in investigating the long-ignored traditions of the common folk. In all of their work they hoped to be able to raise the national spirit of the Germans, and to restore it to its rightful place within its own land.

This brings us back to an important point: the old ways did not really die. It is clear that they, like Sleeping

Beauty, were only put under a spell of sleep while awaiting their noble awakening. In remote regions of all the Teutonic lands the old ways continued to be preserved in folk ways and folk tales. These old ways then became the material for study and clarification by the academics. In this we see how, in the larger scheme of things, the scholar and the old wives of the country have worked together to forge a pillar of the Teutonic Renaissance.

It was not only among scholars that the new interest in national traditions was aroused. Artists as well turned their attention inward and produced works reflective of the new "Teutonicism." (The term Teuton-icism seems here more appropriate than Roman-ticism.) Chief among these artists, at least in the influence he had, was Richard Wagner. In the late 1800s Wagner's personalized vision of the Teutonic past, both ancient (in the Ring Cycle) and medieval (in the Grail Cycle), were to be the mythic foundation for many a Teutonicist. These must, however, be taken as essentially the personal artistic creations of Wagner himself and not as re-tellings of the ancient myth-forms.

By the beginning of the 20th century, the groundwork had been laid in the academic field, in the artistic field, and in the field of popular culture for a serious Teutonic Renaissance. Especially in Germany, but also in England and Scandinavia, groups with Teutonic roots were springing up. The movement was truly one of "grass-roots," coming as it did from all sectors of the political spectrum. The appeal of the timeless values of the ancestors was almost universal among the folk.

There was a mass movement, centered in Germany, which consisted of many groups loosely associated under the term *Deutschbewegung* ("Germanic Movement"); their members eventually numbered in the millions. At the same time, in Austria and Germany, there were the *Armanen*, a runo-mystical movement springing from the teachings of the Viennese mystic Guido von List. A list published in 1914 of books and magazines intended to be a guide through the maze of these movements takes up 33 pages.

In England, youth movements and social-reform movements of all kinds were being based on Teutonic principles. It is a little-known fact that the "Boy Scouts" were originally founded by Baden-Powell as a part of a general movement for the regeneration of ancient Anglo-Saxon values and traditions, and that these aims were eventually subverted by the established church and state in England. Even then it was typical for those who would subvert the true tendencies in these movements to turn the attention to "American Indian" traditions. Because this was exotic and really had nothing to do with the boys in reality, it could be used as a tool to infuse all sorts of nonsense. When one is focused on the traditions of one's own ancestors, all sorts of powerful (and for the church and state very dangerous) results can arise. A few years ago, Danish Boy Scouts began to experiment with "Viking traditions," building Viking ships and the like. This was shut down by the international body governing the Scouts because such practices would foster a sense of national, rather than the desired international, sensibilities of the organization!

It was, however, in Germany where the strongest voices for a true Teutonic revival rose. In the list of books and magazines published in 1914 mentioned above, it is important to note the date—just before the First World War. Later revisionists of the period insist that the longing for a heroic Teutonic past was somehow a result of Germany's "defeat" in the Great War. But clearly the facts show that the *Deutschbewegung* was already strong and multifaceted even before the war began. To be sure, defeat spurred these feelings, as the Germans looked for radical solutions to their problems.

It is essentially true that the rise of the National

Socialist political movement was closely intertwined with the rise of the "Teutonic Movement." There were attempts on both sides to "use" the other to their benefit. Members of the Nazi leadership, especially Adolf Hilter and Heinrich Himmler, as well as masses of their rank-and-file supporters, were generational products of a time in which the notion of ancient Teutonic values and virtues (usually misunderstood) were held up as ideals. To some extent it might be said that the Nazis used the symbolism of the ancient Teutonic past—in the runic *Hakenkreuz* (swastika)—as tools of manipulation. It can be said with equal validity that they were manipulated by these symbols. In any event, once the Nazis gained and began to consolidate their power, they systematically suppressed the entire *Deutschbewegung*; but because the Nazis had made so much use of Teutonic symbolism and rhetoric for purposes of propaganda, the distinctions between the long-standing, centuries-old Teutonic Rebirth and the National Socialist German Workers Party were blurred, to say the least. Unfortunately this fact is often lost even on current proponents of the Renaissance.

Without doubt, the Nazi episode set the course of the Teutonic Rebirth back at least a hundred years. Those who want to see a true rebirth in the ways of the ancestors would be wise to see the Nazi episode for what it was: an essentially Christian-inspired running amok of the militaristic second function—the uncontrolled warrior mentality—which led to a senseless destruction of our progress.

The whole study of and interest in things Teutonic became virtually tabu in the years following the Second World War. (The result of this can still be felt at all levels of society today, in academia as well as in the "neo-pagan" culture.) It wasn't until some two-and-a-half decades after the war that the Teutonic Rebirth began to make its first slow steps back into the realm of consciousness. What had been an awakened giant had been dealt something close to a knockout blow; now, it was coming to, and beginning to shake the cobwebs out of its head.

In North America, England, Iceland, and in Germany the renewal of the rebirth process caught new fire in the early 1970s. In Iceland the Asatrurmenn, under their *allsherjargodhi* the poet Sveinbjörn Beinteinsson, revived the old religion and gained official recognition for it. In Germany the old organizations were receiving new life as well. In North America the Ásatrú Free Assembly (AFA) was founded by Stephen A. McNallen. It strove for the establishment of a full spectrum of Northern religious expression. Other groups in North America also sought to give an outlet to various forms of the Northern Way. England saw the restoration of the Odinic Rite under the able leadership of John Yeowell.

In the lands where the Troth is at home, in North America, the banner of the true way was for a long time perceived to be held by the AFA. It seemed to hold out the best hope for an eventual evolution of a multifaceted confederation of interests true to the elder ways. However, as the organization grew, it was unable to maintain its integrity, and in 1987 it was dissolved. It is in this event that the roots of the Ring of Troth as an organization are to be found. The true rebirth is not dependent on any one organization. But when the banner falls, it must be taken up again. The Ring of Troth again raises the banner high—for all to see and for all to strive toward.

5

The Shape of the World

> *Nine worlds I know,*   the nine abodes
> *of the great world tree*   the ground beneath.
>   (Voluspá, stanza 2)

     Every religion has a view of the world: how it came
into being, what its true shape and nature are, and so forth.
These matters are not just the concern of idle mystics. If
you doubt it, look at how questions of cosmology shape the
political debate of a modern Western democracy such as
the United States. Questions surrounding education, such
as "creationism" versus evolution; women's rights and
abortion; and many other issues can essentially be traced
back to Judeo-Christian cosmological lore of how the world
and its inhabitants came into being and what their proper
configuration is. If we shift our worldview, our cosmology,
we can shift the whole field of debate, and thereby alter the
world. We will return to some of these points later, but
right now the largest question looms before us: "What was
the beginning of all things?," as Gangleri puts it in the *Prose
Edda*.
     The true man or woman can read the surviving accounts
of the ancient Teutonic lore of how the world came into
being in the *Poetic* and *Prose Eddas*, and can get other hints

at the grand scheme in a variety of other sources. All true folk are encouraged to read and meditate on these tales, as each person will win new personal wisdom from them each time he or she does so. But in order to draw the quickening waters from these wells of wisdom, one must have a basic understanding of what the grand scheme is.

What is clear in all accounts of Teutonic cosmogony (accounts of the birth of the ordered worlds) is that there was a great space filled with undifferentiated and unordered force and form. The old Norse word for this is *Ginnungagap*: the space (*gap*) was filled with numinous power (*ginnung*). The *ginn* part of the world is the same that we have in English: be-ginning. This is far from a "void" as it is usually understood. It is vital essence, waiting for a process of change and shaping to occur.

Within this beginning there arose a polarization. Parts of the substance of the chaotic state divided into two extremes, fire and ice, or fire and water which became ice. Between these two extremes, a magnetic force of attraction arose, and the two extremes were attracted to one another. As they came closer and closer to one another, their differences did not lessen, but rather intensified, so that when they did meet in the middle there was a great release of force. Poets can tell of this process in one language, mystics in another, and modern scientists in yet another. But what is essentially being described is an impersonal process of the formation of cosmic order out of the polarized mass of energy. The language which this, that or the other person uses to describe it may differ, but it is a timeless and eternally valid way of looking at the origins of the cosmos.

Once the first stage of the crystallization process had been completed, various entities, or specialized functions within the cosmos, began to take shape. Again these were essentially of two kinds, the proto-zoomorphs (exemplified by Adhumbla, the cosmic bovine), and the protoanthropomorphs (exemplifed by Ymir, the cosmic giant). These two streams of being were united in the gods Woden, Willi, and Weh as the offspring of Borr (descended from Buri, shaped by the cosmic bovine) and Bestla (descended from Ymir). This was the birth of the possibility for true consciousness in the cosmos. Again, the lore and myth may seem complex and sometimes bewildering, but what is essential is the understanding that the gods arose out of a synthesis of the polarized streams on an organic level, just as the basic material of the cosmos had arisen as a synthesis of the polarized streams on a material level. What we see over and over again is the portrayal of latent patterns being made manifest through a process of polarization between two extremes and their synthesis in the middle ground between them. This pattern of thought and of action is the most essential factor of Teutonic thinking.

The gods, the æsir, and the forces of consciousness must complete or at least continue with the process of shaping the cosmos. (It will be noted that we avoid the use of the word "creation," as it implies the creation of something out of nothing, which is foreign to the Teutonic way of thinking, or perhaps foreign to thinking, period. *Ex nihilo* creation is, of course, the cosmology of the Christians.) These gods perform the first act of sacrifice when they slay the giant Ymir and reshape the universe in a more ordered fashion from the parts of his cosmic body. The gods of consciousness shape the nine worlds, which are patterned on the framework of the cosmic tree, Yggdrasill. Then comes into being nine worlds or dimensions of being, and infinite multiplicities between and among them. In these dimensions dwell the gods and goddesses, and all the wights and beings of all the worlds.

The cosmos is an unfinished thing. The gods continue to work on it, and in this work their chief partners are the true men and women of Midgard. Here it is clear that along

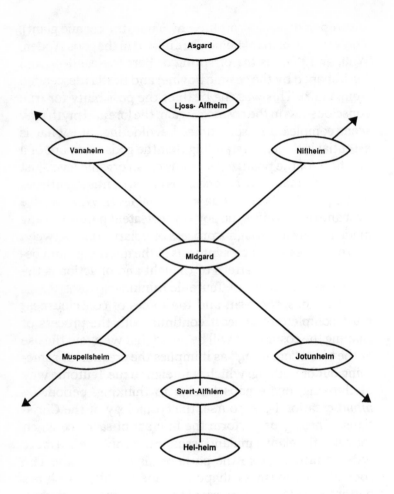

The Nine Worlds of Yggdrasill

with the notion of the give-and-take between two extremes there is a more complex pattern ordered by the cycle of the number nine. This is an infinite cycle of shaping and transformation governed by an eternal return to the essential truth of its own self. Again, this might seem to be the stuff of mysticism, and it can be, but it is also a form of down-to-earth common sense. How else again to explain the weird fact that you are reading these words?

What of mankind's role in all of this? What is mankind, essentially? These are among the most important questions that can be asked, we being men and women, after all. Human beings were shaped by the gods Woden, Willi, and Weh from the organic material of trees; men from the ash tree, women from the elm. The worlds were shaped along the organic patterns exemplified by trees, and so too was humanity. This is why each person contains a microcosm corresponding to the macrocosm. Humans were shaped out of the same stuff from which the gods were shaped, and eventually the gods also planted the very seed of their being in the womb of humanity, so that the race of gods and the race of men has become inexorably bound together. For us there is a bond of mutual dependence between gods and men—we share the same wyrd.

The message of all of Germanic cosmological lore is fairly clear when read with an open mind. The "events" described are guided by a combination of natural processes and conscious intervention. The natural processes are characterized by the interaction of two extremes, while the workings of conscious intervention are guided by a nine-fold pattern leading to infinite multiplicities. Humanity is a full and responsible partner in the process of shaping the cosmos. Men and women are made of the same kind of stuff; while the quality of the material is the same, their natures are different. Also, men and women are endowed by the gods with the same spiritual qualities or gifts. The contrasts between this and the Judeo-Christian mythology is stark, for those who would bother to attempt to compare them.

We, like the gods, can win or we can lose. We can choose a heroic existence of eternal life and struggle, or one of death and desolation.

6

Lore

Lore is that which has been left behind, like the tracks of an animal we are hunting. "Tradition" is the more usual word we now use for this. Tradition is that which is handed down from generation to generation. That which is actually transmitted may be considered twofold: 1) the lore itself, that is, information of some kind usually expressed in verbal form, and 2) power, that is, the energy or spiritual ability and wisdom which is usually passed directly from a lore-master to his or her apprentice. It cannot be denied that a large number of well-known traditions emphasize the direct, unbroken line of descent of their teachings and their power from some primary master(s), or even from a god. This is usually traced to some historical time and place where the tradition began. The old forces of Christianity claim that their bishops were in a direct line of initiatory descent ("apostolic succession") from the twelve apostles chosen by Jesus to spread his dogmas. This way of doing things is really not enviable, because it tends to maintain rigid forms in a futile attempt to combat the evolutionary process. Furthermore, it is decidedly dualistic, as it posits an external source for this power, which is given "from above" to "those below." It might also be pointed out that this "apostolic succession" has been historically proven to be an absolute forgery.

This process presupposes a single source of legitimate lore and power, an idea found in many other religious and magical systems. Many schools of ritual magic(k) also make a fetish of the idea of a direct line of initiatory tradition with its ultimate source among "secret chiefs." In cases of this kind we usually find that some universalist ideology is either openly advocated or lurks somewhere just below the surface. It should not be denied that direct, face-to-face teaching—master to apprentice—is the most effective way of transmitting both lore and power. However, the mode by which the "master" obtains the lore and power at his or her disposal is often varied. Many of the revivalist neo-pagan movements of the 19th and 20th centuries have perhaps found it in their best interests to fabricate "apostolic successions" for themselves. If we look at this idea more closely, we see that this may have been done more for superficial psychological effect than for any other reason.

The elder lore of the troth was not rigid. It did not seek to preserve a codified, petrified set of dogmatic forms throughout all eternity—such as Christians attempt with their concept of the unchanging "Word of God." It is therefore ironic that, at its very core, the troth of an Icelander of the Viking Age was unchanged from the troth of his most distant ancestors who came roaring out of the steppes 5,000 years earlier. This is due to an unbound flow of lore rather than to a codified set of dogmas or even a consciously agreed-upon tradition.

Many Indo-European traditions, for example that of the Celtic Druids and Indian Brahmans, developed along lines which emphasized a codified lore taught in schools. But the tradition of the troth remained for the most part in the realm of "natural tradition," and was constantly in a state of flux. Various tribes probably had different traditions

regarding a priesthood, which would account for the varying reports we get about such traditions from the Roman
historians. Some probably had a true priest class, while
others had none. In all cases they were certainly respond-
ing to prevailing conditions in the most effective ways at
the disposal of the tradition.

The transmission of runelore would be a case in point.
When we look at the runic tradition, we see that all evidence
points to an ancient network through which rune wisdom
was quickly and uniformly passed. Therefore, there must
have been a specialized subculture throughout all Teutonic tribal territories which carried on this tradition.
This was most likely the Wodenic priesthood and/or skalds.
But even this tradition was probably not one with a set of
complex ritual forms and dogmas. The technical aspects of
the runic system formed the core of this tradition, but its
individual characteristics were most certainly formulated
within various tribal frameworks.

The runic tradition was one which gave a particular
shape and "quality" to the natural, genetically inherited
tribal force, which through this shape and quality could be
more easily communicated to others. In other words, the
runic tradition would, by today's decadent standards,
probably baffle most people with its simplicity. A single
key provided to a simple stock of symbols housed in a
naturally integrated psyche will open the door of a true
tradition. In the words of someone who was an initiate in
this tradition:

> Then I began to grow   and gain in insight,
>   to wax also in wisdom:
> one word led on   to another word,
> one work led on   to another work.
>   *(Hávamál, stanza 141)*

The natural mode of access to this inner tradition has been suppressed by an unnatural universalist dogma of guilt and alienation. The shape of the true lore was in many cases radically altered. The living masters who held the spiritual keys to this hoard of lore were either killed or eventually prevented from transmitting their teachings. Society was altered so as to be inhospitable to the holy gods and more pleasing to Christ. Do we have anything left of this inner tradition to draw from today? Again, let us break this down in the two-fold way introduced above.

1) Lore (Form of Tradition)

The hard evidence available to us about the old Germanic religion is quite extensive, and with the work of ingenious modern scholars in the fields of archeology, linguistics, and comparative religion we may begin to rebuild, on a firm and intellectually sound foundation, that which has been lost of the outward form of the troth and its traditions. We actually have more than enough of the core symbols available to us with which to re-form the old ways. The primary responsibility of present-day loremasters is to focus on the true and basic sources before flying off to exotically inspired solutions.

2) Power (Content of the Tradition)

In the ancient form of the troth, the passing of power from master to apprentice formed an important part of the cult—and this direct line has been cut. This is not as serious as it would appear to be from the viewpoint of one who believes in a single transcendent source of spiritual power, for each individual has the ability to gain access to at least a portion of that natural in-dwelling power. This power has come down to him or her by virtue of the fact that he or she is literally descended from the gods, without any "transgression" against these gods. Now, if these individuals pool their spiritual powers and mold them into a transmittable form, and succeed in passing them from one generation to the next, the troth will truly be reborn. The real power structure we are talking about has always lived within us, and has been handed down, constantly being re-formed, from parent to child all the way from the beginning of our folk. This is the "natural succession," which has been in part suppressed by an alien creed. But it is still present and it is still responsive to its symbols if one will only venture forth! The power belongs to those who dare.

There is another interesting aspect of this "problem," an examination of which may result in demonstrating that it is not at all a disadvantage. The birth-life-death-rebirth cycle is central to the troth. Between every death and rebirth there is a period of gestation—this is valid for plants, animals, humans, gods, and ideas. In order to survive Ragnarök, Woden planted his seed to be reborn in Vidharr, so that he might avenge his own death and be born back into the world, or to survive in the renewed world on the Shining Plain. This process may also describe what is transpiring with regard to the tradition of the troth. The past 800 to 1,000 years have been a gestation period in which the power of the tradition has been increasing in preparation for its full rebirth in an even greater spiritual capacity. Such a reading is consistent with the greater Teutonic world-view of the sacredness of flux and the birth-life-death-rebirth cycle, which stands in contrast to the steady-state, linear conceptions of other traditions.

The True must take that lore which has been dealt us, dig deep into our souls with the tools given by the gifts of the gods, work together in the true spirit of the troth and shape this into a tradition founded on the old way and on the re-born power. Most importantly we must hand it down to our children, to the next generation, for then and only then will the tradition truly be reborn—for they will be able to know fully that it never really died.

We do have enough lore upon which to base a true Teutonic Rebirth. But we do bear a responsibility to focus on the Teutonic tradition first and foremost before flying around looking for meaning in exotic, if perhaps (unfortunately) more familiar doctrines. The essential power-source is one which is forever with us—in-dwelling and indestructible. We *have* the tradition, for we *are* the tradition. If we again dare to take up the plough, the sword and the wand, the power will surge up from our souls and flow along the elder patterns in our minds.

7

The Way of Doing

More than a way of thought or belief, the Troth is a way of doing or being. In most religions, or in philosophies bordering on religions, we can speak of the *ideo*logy of the system, that is, the teachings concerning its ideas. With the Troth we should perhaps more rightly speak of its *practico*logy, that is, teachings concerning its practices or things a true man or woman does. The true essence of a religious or philosophical system is seen in what its practitioners do, not in what they say, or in the rationale of their actions. Action is therefore what is essential in the Troth. Action is the surest and highest measurement of truth and right.

From this do not jump to the conclusion that thought cannot be action. It can. However, not all thought is action. To be a true action, a thought must be an act of conscious will. These acts are not readily observable by all, and are open to various interpretations; they are therefore considered of secondary rank among the true.

There are three kinds of doing. Two of these are of primary importance: day-to-day actions and participation in the Great Blessings of the Year. The third kind is willed mental action.

Day-to-day actions and their disciplined guidance are

treated more fully in chapter 22. The exact standards of right actions are determined by the individual in interaction with the bonds of fellowship he or she has made. What is essential here is that the standard of measurement is found in what one does rather than in what one thinks or believes. It is not enough to say about a man: "He has his heart in the right place." He must have his hand and arm in the right place as well.

Beyond the day-to-day acts of the true, it is their holy responsibility to participate in the Great Blessings of the Year. This is a higher form of action. In this kind of action the true man or woman is able to act in a "realm of being" common to all the gods and ancestors. From a purely "religious" standpoint, these acts of participation in the Great Blessings are the central acts of troth.

In most of the living, vital religions around the world today, most of the followers simply act out of a sense of tradition and spend little time brooding over the whys and wherefores of the religion. This is quite natural. There are, however, a number of people who out of personal interest or passion wish to delve deeper into the lore. Of course, this is the mandatory responsibility of the priesthood in any religion, but it should not be limited to such a body. In actual fact, mental acts are the equal of physical acts. However, they cannot be measured, and cannot be used to measure the troth of a man or woman. It is for this reason that they are considered to be of second rank in the general Troth. Part of the reason for this is to ensure against the rise of an "inquisition mentality," in which a man's "faith" can be called into question just because this or that individual does not agree with his views. If he acts true, he is true.

As a general rule in all things, both ancient and modern, involving the Troth, it will be seen that doing comes before understanding. This is really a natural state of affairs. The reason for this may or may not be obvious. Before gaining true understanding of a thing, one must have experienced it as completely as possible. If one had to "understand" the mechanics of how human beings are able to move before trying to walk, no one would have ever been able to take their first steps. The practice of the Troth, like walking, is an act natural to humanity—but like walking it is something that must be learned through the channels of traditions.

8

Giving

Better it is not to bid,   than to bless overmuch,
aye looks a gift always for gain;
'tis better unasked   than offered overmuch ...
(Hávamál 145)

Giving, or yielding, gifts to the gods and goddesses of the Troth and getting their gifts in return is the essence of sacrifice. There is probably no more misunderstood concept, or one about which there are more misconceptions, than sacrifice. Most of these misconceptions come from a lack of knowledge about our own ways of sacrificing, coupled with a confusion between what we mean by it and what other "sacrificing" cultures meant by it. When most people hear about sacrifice nowadays, examples that might come to mind would include beautiful virgins being thrown into angry volcanos, the hearts of the best of the youth being torn out and offered to the sun god, or animals being consumed in the fires on the altar of Yahweh in the Temple in Jerusalem. People think of "sacrifice" as being a useless, superstitious "throwing away" of the best of things to a non-existent god or his priests. Such a concept of sacrifice deserves to die out.

What the Troth has always meant by giving, or yielding, gifts to the gods is something very different. In Teutonic as well as in general Indo-European culture, sacrifice has always meant giving to the gods what the gods find useful and of benefit, and taking for mankind what mankind finds useful or of benefit. Sacrifice is the exchange of gifts binding men and gods together in a bond of mutual good.

The terminology for "sacrifice" used in the Troth is telling. Before exploring that, let us look at the word "sacrifice." It is a Latin word, and really means simply "to make sacred," or "to make separate from the profane world." To make something sacred is to send it to the realm of the gods, there to act as a sort of gift and message to them. To this gift the gods must of need respond. This is the philosophy of all Indo-European sacrifice, be it Indian, Iranian, Roman, Greek, Celtic, or Teutonic.

In the working terminology of the Troth we speak of giving, yielding, or offering. Each of these words indicate the idea of giving a gift to the gods. The Old English or Old Norse ancestors of these words were, by the way, used in a religious sense as well. Another word we use is "blessing." This literally and originally meant "to sprinkle with blood." Technically, this is the sprinkling of cult objects and the folk with the vivifying, hallowing power of the blood of a sacrificial animal. The same terminology is also used for making similar blessings with water or other liquid offerings.

Animal sacrifice, according to the ancient way, is not normally practiced today in the Troth. But it is important to understand what the nature of this animal sacrifice was so that its principles can be known and used. An animal sacrifice was, to our way of thinking now, more akin to a sacralized barbecue than to the useful slaughter of livestock. In days of yore, the meat of the animal killed would serve as the sanctified essence of the god or goddess, which was then consumed by the gathered folk. This was an act of ritual "communion" in the literal sense. The animal shared an essential link with the god or goddess to which it was dedicated: the horse to Woden, the goat to Thunar, the boar to Frey and the sow to Freya. (This really explains why the eating of horse-meat was so strongly forbidden by the Christians!) By eating the hallowed meat, the true folk became more closely linked with their gods. Certain parts of the animals—those parts which the folk found little to their use or liking, such as the heads or lower legs—might then be given or returned to the gods. Only these parts would typically be "sacrificed" in the sense known to most people, being burned, or deposited in holy wells.

It is also noteworthy that it was important to the priests that the sacrificial animal not suffer in the process of the blessing. They were killed quickly and humanely; techniques of slowly and painlessly suffocating the animals were even developed. This is reflected in old technical terms such as Old English *swebban* and Old Norse *soa*, which literally mean "to put to sleep." The reason for this is obvious: the animal is a manifestation of the god, and is therefore approached with reverence and love.

A very different attitude is reflected in the old Teutonic practices of human sacrifice, but this too is important to understand. The ancient Teutons never sacrificed their "best and brightest," or their first-born, or anything of the sort. Human sacrifices were most usually made of criminals and of prisoners of war—those whom the society had to rid itself of in any event. Simply put, human sacrifice was a form of sacralized "capital punishment." The victim of human sacrifice was someone who had put the realm of the gods out of balance in some profound way by their own acts. To correct this imbalance their lives had to be forfeited.

Although we may find many of these concepts of no use today, it is imperative that we understand our tradition for what it was, and not let some superstitious representative of Christianity try to tell us what cruel barbarians our ancestors were. This is especially so since the spiritual roots of Christianity do go back to Middle Eastern cults that practiced ritual sacrifice not only of animals but also occasionally of the people's children.

The ritual norms of the Troth today mainly involve the use of hallowed liquids, mead (Kavisir's Blood), ale, or beer. These substances were also used in ancient times. Essentially, the ritual techniques and the wisdom surrounding their right use are the same in all cases.

In the blessing, the gods and mankind touch each other. The blessings are a way of intermingling the essences of divinity and humanity. Why this is done should be obvious. First, it is done simply because it is the right thing to do. Here the word "right" is used in a special religious sense. What is right is what maintains the right and natural order of the cosmos that ensures a hospitable place where gods and men can exist. The blessings—which mankind is responsible for carrying out—help maintain the cosmic order first instituted by the Ases at the dawn of time. Without this order we cannot exist, and the gods cannot exist. With more blessings, the quality of human existence will improve; with fewer blessings it will degenerate. Thus is the wisdom of offerings.

Another reason blessings are performed is to exchange specific gifts with the gods and goddesses. We offer a certain kind of gift and we will get some gift in return. This return gift will correspond to the character of the god or goddess. Because these kinds of gifts always require a response of some kind from the divine realm, it is wise not to do this unless absolutely necessary, or at special seasonal times when it is right to do so. One should be moderate in sacrifice, because such gifts always look for gain. As one might wear out the soil in a field by over-cultivating it, one can also wear out one's welcome among the gods with too many gifts.

A third reason for participating in or performing blessings is to simply and deeply *be* with the gods and goddesses—to be among them in order to communicate with them directly and in an essential way. This is most profoundly experienced in the part of the blessing which involves the consumption of the hallowed drink or meal. The more this is done (within the bounds of the second reason), the more like the gods one can become, and the more power the gods will have in Midgard.

The wisdom of giving is threefold. It ensures right order, that we have a place to live and work; it provides for a channel through which we receive gifts from, and give gifts to, the gods; and it gives us a way to raise our beings to new heights.

9

The Holy Year

From the south the sun,   by the side of the moon,
heaved her right hand   over heaven's rim;
the sun knew not   what seat she had,
the stars knew not   what stead they held,
the moon knew not   what might he had.

Then gathered together   the gods to rede
the holy hosts,   and held speech;
to night and new moon   their names they gave,
the morning named,   and midday also,
forenoon and evening   to order the year.

(Völuspá 5-6)

Every culture orders time. The way time is ordered gives us insight into the inner world of the folk. Today we mainly order our time on a daily and weekly basis, according to corporate work schedules: nine to five, five days a week, with a two-day weekend, week in and week out. For the ancient Teutonic folk, the year and the month were far more important than the day or the week. Furthermore, these divisions of time were ruled by holy principles, which were symbols in time of happenings going on both within the soul and within nature.

What we call "time" is only really discernible through the movement of bodies—the Sun, the Moon, the Earth,

51

the stars above. Happenings in nature, such as the appearance of the first violet or robin in spring, coincide with some movement in the heavens—the Sun rising over a certain holy stead—and about that time a young man's fancy turns to love (or war). This threefold happening, on Earth, in the heavens, and in the soul, is seen as meaningful and holy. Here we have the basis of the holy year, and why it is so important in the Troth.

In the days and nights of yore the many tribes of the Teutonic folk had various traditions concerning time and its ordering. Some used sophisticated observations of the heavens to determine when their holy events were to take place, while others relied more on Earth-bound happenings. For example, one occurrence for determining the tide for the Easter-blessing might be the first full Moon after the spring equinox; another tribe might use the formula of the first full Moon after the appearance of the first blossom of spring in some holy grove or field. The first formula shows some astronomical sophistication, but in some places it may not have given a date that corresponded to the events in earthly nature with which the Easter-blessing is supposed to coincide. The other formula shows little astronomical sophistication, but ensures that the organic events of the Easter-tide are actually present. Both formulas will probably result in the same date for the actual workings of the springtime blessings. In both cases, the full Moon is important—for the name of the Moon means the "measurer," or the one who metes out time with his phases and movements. The *mon-th* really means "a measurement of the Moon."

Just as our ancient forebears came to terms with their year and lunar phases in accordance with the socio-economic realities of their world, thus making them holy and meaningful, so are we challenged to do the same in our world. It may, on occasion, be desirable to take the modern workday/weekend schedule into account when setting dates for holy events. It may be better, and more true, to have a leisurely and convivial time with other good folk and true, than to rush about on a workday night with little time or energy to appreciate the holyness of the tide and fellowship. At the same time, we must remember that in the ancient orderings of the holy year there is a timeless meaning that even in our modern world continues to shine through. Why do we have our most important festivals in the fall (Thanksgiving) and winter (Yule), and why have Hallowe'en and St. Valentine's Day assumed increasing importance in recent years? These are but pale reflections of the elder orderings of the holy year.

In the Teutonic mind there are really only two "seasons" or tides of the year: winter and summer. These are marked by two of the greatest blessings: the Yule-tide at midwinter (beginning on or about December 21 and lasting twelve nights), and Midsummer (on or about June 21).

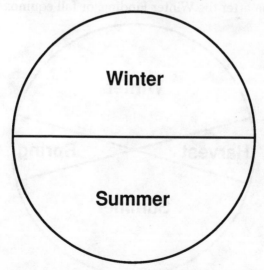

Figure 9.1: Twofold Division of the Year

At the periods of transition from one time of year to another, from summer to winter and from winter to summer, there are also two great blessings. These are not really seasons unto themselves, but are rather shorter tides in which the event of transition is the most important happening. This is reflected in the language. We see that "spring" is that time when nature begins to "spring forth" and come again into bloom; once this tide is past, summer is present. "Fall" is only that time when the leaves begin to fall; once they have fallen, winter is upon us. The fact that these events take place at different times in different places strengthens the tradition of having these festivals somewhat mobile, and not fixed to a regular "mechanical event" in the heavens. The tide of the spring festival, Easter, is reckoned as mentioned above—the first full Moon after the spring equinox, or Summer Finding. But some might want to celebrate Easter on the equinox itself. The fall festival of Harvest would likewise be reckoned to come on the first full Moon after the Winter Finding, or fall equinox.

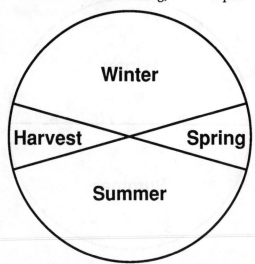

Figure 9.2: The Tides of Fall and Spring in the Year

Other festivals fall between these tides. One of the three Greatest Blessings of the Troth comes between the Winter Finding and the Yule-tide, and is called the Winter Nights. In the ancient North, this fell on or about the present October 14th. Between the Yule-tide and Easter, there falls a holy day known as Disting, during which local legal assemblies (*things*) gathered and markets were held. Between Easter and Midsummer were May Eve and May Day. Later the Great Things, or national assemblies, were held between Midsummer and Winter Finding. Except for Yule and Midsummer all of the holy tides mentioned here were held during the full phase of the Moon. Usually they would start on the night just before the full Moon and last for three nights. The holy calendar of the Troth therefore appears as illustrated on page 56.

The Teutonic peoples divided the heavens into eight parts or directions. The year is thus divided by the holy days, and is further subdivided by the months, or Moons. In ancient times every tribe seems to have had a slightly different way of doing this and to have had various names for the months as well. The ritual timing for the working of the blessings and festivals of the Troth are further outlined in Part Two of this book.

What is essential to realize is that the year represents a cycle, an ever-turning wheel of time. In this wheel all great things return; but it takes the right deeds of mankind, working together with the holy works of the gods and goddesses and all in harmony with nature, to ensure the continuance of the right order of the world. Again we see the need for the harmonious workings of men, gods and nature.

As we go around the wheel of the year we make holy space in time for communion with the gods. Each stead in time has its special task. When in these holy spaces in time, the true man or woman is in a holy state of being. This is

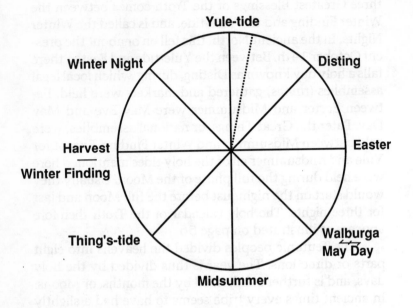

Yule-tide

Disting

Winter Night

Easter

Harvest
Winter Finding

Thing's-tide

Walburga
May Day

Midsummer

Figure 9.3: The Eightfold Division of the Holy Year

why peace (frith) is the law during these times. The eight spokes of the wheel of the year give us the basic framework for the ritual calendar of the Troth. Within the general framework, however, many variables are possible. There are quite a number of other holy days and festivals not mentioned here. Some of these are traditional and some have been newly created in various Ásatrú/Odinist groups. In current Troth practice, it is quite common for kindreds, hearths, or garths to remove a holy day to a Saturday or Sunday in order that the full measure of the festival can be taken.

The inner meaning of the wheel of the year is as deep and real as it was when it was used to guide the deeds of our ancestors in their works as farmers and herdsmen. It must be understood that the cycles represent what is right. By harmonizing with them, and yielding gifts at the right times, the folk get back their right rewards as the gifts of the gods and nature. The wheel of the year is the cycle of eternal growth, of becoming, of evolution if you will. By understanding and experiencing its cycle, true folk understand all other cycles.

10

The Folk

*One's self only knows   what is near one's heart,
                each reads but himself aright;
no sickness seems   to a sound mind worse
           than to have lost all liking for life.
                              (Hávamál 95)*

The Troth is the religion of the people in whose tongue the word is spoken. Each people of the world has a religion that is natural to them, a religion with which they are at home. Sadly, these native religions have been in retreat before the monolithic and spiritually imperialistic religions. However, as long as the ethnic identity of a people remains, the possibility for the rebirth of its true ethical way remains also.

Christianity is a false and artificial overlay. This central fact is perhaps more responsible than anything else for the cultural schizophrenia that our world suffers from today. We instinctively know what our natural pathways are, but because we as a culture have adopted as an established standard something that runs counter to these natural inclinations, we have set ourselves up in an eternal conflict with ourselves.

The Troth simply says: "Come back to the troth of thy forebears." In the Troth, the true man or woman is simply going back to a way that worked for his or her folk for

59

thousands of years before the advent of the artificial overlay of Christianity. The Troth does not ask someone to get into something that has not already been proven over aeons. It is not some exotic and foreign cult (such as Christianity is/was) that has never been practiced in this culture. In many ways the return to the Troth is a return to one's own heart. The essence of this return is the rejection of exotic forms of thinking, and the re-establishment of our own true ways.

The Troth is our own folk-religion. This means that it is the religion that is particular to this folk, to this ethnic group. We seek first and foremost to delve deeply into the long-neglected pathways of our ancestors, to learn their lore, and to follow their examples. Again, doing that which has been done before is a profound truth of our folk; it is the very root of our code of laws even today. That which is right is that which has been done before. In returning to its principles on a religious basis a person would only be doing what is truly right and lawful.

The great psychologist Carl Jung, in an essay entitled "Wotan," crafted an effective metaphor in reference to the mysterious way in which the old gods of our people remain, and can again become active in our world:

> *Archetypes are like riverbeds which dry up when the water deserts them, but which it can find again at any time. An archetype is like an old water-course along which the water of life has flowed for centuries, digging a deep channel for itself. The longer it has flowed in this channel, the more likely it is that sooner or later the water will return to its old bed.*

This truly says what needs to be said about how the gods and goddesses of our ancestors have always been with us, and how easily they can return if we will but quicken them. These deities are like a secret code present in the very fiber of our being. Other folk carry other codes which are right for them; our code, simply and for no other reason than it is OURS, is right for us. In some ways, following the Troth can be said to be the "path of least resistance" in religion, because in the Troth true folk are following along already established internal patterns—whereas in following unnatural, unprepared pathways, the follower has to dig his own way with little to guide him but the dogmas of external sources.

In the simplest terms, the Troth teaches those who would be true to hold dear that which is near—to seek the holy in that which is close at hand. We must be wise enough to see that that which we have been told is "our heritage" is often nothing but a Middle Eastern cult which has insinuated itself within our own culture. First these blinders must be removed. Then, and only then, will that which is truly near and therefore dear to your heart be shown.

One's home is best   *though a hut it be:*
    there a man is master and lord;
his heart doth bleed   *who has to beg*
    the meat for his every meal.
         (Hávamál 37)

11

The Gods and Goddesses

> *Then Gangleri asked: "Who are the gods men ought to trust in?"*
>
> *High-One replied: "The divine gods are twelve in number."*
>
> *Just-as-High added: "The goddesses are no less holy and no less mighty."*
>
> *(Gylfaginning, ch. 20)*

The subject of the gods and goddesses is difficult, actually impossible, to address in a work of this kind. This is because the gods and goddesses as personal manifestations invite deep personal relationships with true men and women. Each of these relationships is unique, and no general, universally correct statements can be made on the gods and goddesses at this living level. What can be said is that the gods and goddesses are *real*, that there are many of them, that they are ordered in a sort of divine society, and that they are as dependent upon us for their continuing existence as we are on them for our being.

What are the gods and goddesses? To this question there can be many answers. Much depends on the level of understanding any one true man or woman has at any one time. Real gods, like real people, are not one-dimensional, easily defined and pigeonholed entities. Some understand the gods as pure mental or psychological constructs, some

63

as true living beings, and others as forces of nature. The Troth does not put limits on the levels or types of understandings true folk can reach on this subject. To be true, one must but trust in the gods and goddesses of the folk.

One thing that must be borne in mind is that in the Troth all the gods and goddesses are honored in an even-handed way: each according to its dignity in the ordering of the divinities. Individuals will have their favorite gods and goddesses, and worship them privately and in the open. On an official level all of the gods and goddesses are often worshipped together.

The idea of having many gods and goddesses may seem "primitive" to some, but it really is "ultra-modern" (and actually timeless). Today, in our post-Christian world, we are already quite naturally falling back on our old system of many gods. In a so-called pluralistic society we allow for many life-styles, value systems, and so forth. For each of these there is very often and quite naturally an icon or symbol of some kind which serves as a focus for that value system. In real terms this is a sign of the god or goddess behind that value system. The various gods and goddesses are to some extent living centers of deep-seated values, within individuals and within the whole culture. Only one example of this will suffice to show what is meant here. It is not by accident that we call our iconic female sex-symbols "goddesses"—for through them is manifested the power of the Lady Freya. Her living form is used to sell everything from automobiles (another divine icon: the horse) to toothpaste. If you need proof of the true existence of the gods and goddesses, look around with open eyes and they will overwhelm you with their presence.

In the elder wisdom, it was known that that which made men and women human was a set of divine gifts given by the gods at the birth of humanity (Völuspá 17-18). Through and within these gifts we know the gods directly, for it is that which we share with them. The gods and goddesses are therefore seen as the divine ancestors. We are, in one way or another, descended from them body and soul. This is also the real reason why, no matter what we do, we cannot really "break with" the gods. Ours is not a "contractual" relationship; it is one of blood. So long as we exist, the gods and goddesses exist.

The names and characteristics of the many gods and goddesses are manifold. At a certain level, different tribal groups had different gods and goddesses, or else gave the ones they had in common differing levels of honor. Each true man and woman is charged with the personal exploration of the gods and goddesses. Their lore must be learned and they must again be honored by those who would be true to them. Each individual true man and woman must find, for him- or herself, the god or goddess (or combination of them in some number) that is right for that individual. It is not necessarily customary for sons and daughters to follow the religious orientation of their fathers and mothers. This is because within the realm of the Troth the varieties of religious experience are infinite.

There are two main classes or families of the gods: the Ases and the Wanes. Their powers intermingle on many levels, since although they are distinct from one another on one level, on another level the Ases have taken in the Wanes to form one vast realm of the gods with two poles of power. In the Ases are centered the powers of consciousness and force under the control of consciousness, while in the Wanes are centered the organic powers of nature. The intermingling of these two poles defines the nature of the human experience; and how they effectively and rightly intermingle and relate to the human experience is the esssence of the Troth.

Of all the gods of the Teutons it must be said that Woden is the highest and most mighty. His might and main is that of the soul and mind. He is the giver of the spiritual gifts that allow us to know and understand ourselves and the world, and this is the root of his supremacy. It is mainly for this reason that he is called the All-Father. He is the god of the runes (mysteries), ecstasy, poetry, magic, death and a hundred other things besides. His names number in the hundreds also, for all that we can name has something of Woden in it. To approach Woden it takes a brave—and perhaps foolhardy—soul. This is because he is as fickle and as mysterious as the workings of our own minds. Woden is the ultimate god of the sovereign power of kings and priests—that power which brings all things, no matter how diverse they seem, together in a meaningful way. But in ancient times, although his primacy was acknowledged, he was not a popular god. Only those few who were chosen followed him, usually to apparent disaster.

Also high and mighty is the god Tiw. He is the god of the rational mind, and rules over our abilities to reason and to come to good judgments. It is his power that is behind the ordering of the rational laws of the cosmos and of human society. Tiw is the god of true law and order. This is also a quality much valued among the sovereign powers. Tiw can only judge and give his favor to that which is right, but our innate trust in our own rightness leads us to call on him for victory. In doing so we make as much a statement of trust in our own selves as we do in Tiw himself. Tiw is also the spirit of giving of the individual self to serve the interests of the whole. This also sets Tiw apart from the masses. His path is a demanding, and sometimes thankless, one.

Among the goddesses the greatest is said to be Frigga. She is the queen of the goddesses and seems to hold them all together in an orderly fashion. She is no simple goddess of fertility, as some might try to make her. Her power holds the social fabric together and she sees to domestic order—

within the realms of the gods as well as in Midgard.

Thunar is the ancient war-god. Although he is not necessarily the main god among all warriors, he eternally holds this position among the gods. He is their chief defender; with his mighty hammer Mjolnir he defends the order of Asgard and Midgard. He is steadfast and true and can be relied on above all other gods. His chief power is that of physical strength. He embodies all the raw physical power in the world in the service of the gods and humanity

Among the Wanes (or Vanir) the goddess Freya is the foremost. Her name means simply "the Lady." She is said to be equal in power with Frigga, but very different in character. In her are embodied the powers of magic, sexual love, cyclic development, and war. She knows the form of magic called seith, which she is said to have taught to Woden. Freya is the mistress of eroticism, which goes beyond "fertility" and into the realm of the power of sexuality itself. Her power in the area of fertility comes from her rulership over the process of things coming into being, growing, and passing away to a new arising. In the turn of the year that leads to wealth and well-being, she works in tandem with her twin brother, Frey. As half of the warriors slain in battle go to the Walhalla to be in Woden's army, the other half go to Freya, to be with her in Folkwang. Among the Wanes, Freya brings all things together in a sort of hidden realm, much as Woden does among the Ases.

The name Frey means simply "the Lord." As Freya is involved with hidden workings among the Wanes, Frey, along with his father/mother Njord, rules over the outer forms. He embodies the manifest powers of wealth, well-being, peace, and pleasure. He is the chief ruler of these things in the world itself. Therefore he is called the God, or Lord, of This-World, so it is easy to see why he and his sister Freya were probably the most popular divinities in the North for the bulk of the people. Among the Wanes, Frey is a reflection of the kingly power embodied in Tiw and Woden among the Ases.

It is most typical for individual true men and women to explore the tales and myths of the gods and goddesses, to meditate on them, and to begin to develop deep inner connections with one or several of the divinities. In nights of yore, of course, this was probably done during childhood, as the tales of the gods and goddesses would have been well known to all. In our present world, however, this learning must be an act of will.

From these brief descriptions it can be seen that the gods and goddesses of the Troth form a profound "community of power" that is quite intricately interwoven. There are threads running through and among the gods and goddesses that show how they are related to one another and how they work together.

The gods and goddesses of our ancestors, whatever they were, still dwell within us. They live as long as we live. They can be put to sleep, they can be silenced, but they cannot be killed, unless the thread or organic being that they set into motion, stretching from generation to generation, be ended. The work of the Troth is the reawakening of the slumbering gods and goddesses. That they have been stirred has already been shown by some unfortunate events of this century. As unpleasant and ineffective as these events proved to be, they are still signs of a fully living divine power. No other "revivalist" movement can claim anything close to these signs of vitality.

We in the Troth must now nurture the already manifest vitality. This is done through the working of blessings, the giving of gifts on a regular basis, and most importantly the development of our own minds and hearts to be able to hear and understand rightly words and ways of the gods and goddesses as they begin to become manifest within us. The horn of the self must be made strong so that it will not burst asunder when the power of the gods flows into it. With each blessing rightly done, with each gift rightly given, we grow ever stronger.

12

The Ladder of Being

The fact that we have many gods and goddesses is shown by the fact that we have many kinds of men and women. But are they all the same, or are they in some ways different from one another? Of course, they are different. There are indeed several kinds of gods and several kinds of men, each corresponding to the other. Each of these kinds, being different in some essential way, has its own special interest to pursue. In order that they all might work together toward the common good, and in order that they might all ensure that their own special purposes be achieved, the gods work in a harmonious relationship that is essential to their very being and survival. The relationship is simply based on the ancient concept of arranging the differing kinds (or qualities) of the gods in a threefold hierarchy. This system of classification is as old as our language. It is the high-higher-highest, the good-better-best of all things.

The gods are arrayed in this way and so is the folk. If knowledge is to be gained, if victories are to be won, if grains are to be sown, grown and harvested, vast—even cosmic-level—teamwork must be brought into play. The various levels and special workings of the gods and goddesses is fairly plain for all to see, and as we hold that the

71

world of men is a shining reflection of the world of the gods and goddesses, it is part of the work of the Troth again to awaken this deep sense of the special and differing tasks of people in the world. Today our world suffers under the curse of same-ness: everything is everything, so nothing is anything. Everybody is somebody, so nobody is anybody.

The divinities of the Troth are essentially divided into three groups which are derived from three great root qualities: sovereignty, force, and generation. Sovereignty is the power of knowing what is right and true and being able to effectively set things into motion to achieve these aims. Force is the physical power to enforce these aims, and to defend the whole from destruction by forces hostile to its aims. Generation is the power to provide for the essential sustenance of the whole, as well as its continuing existence and its pleasure in existing. These qualities must be arranged in just this way: sovereignty must rule over force, and generation must serve the interests of the whole again under the direction of sovereignty. The king commands the warrior; and the farmer, or worker, provides for all. If this is put out of balance in any way, disaster will strike. If the warrior-spirit leads (as it did in Nazi Germany), it will lead to nothing but war and destruction. If the worker-spirit leads (as it does in the Soviet Union), stagnation and rigidity will follow. These are not "natural laws" as such; they are the laws of the divine orders, the laws of the gods ruling in the consciousness of humanity. These laws were imparted to humanity with the threefold gift of Woden - Willi-Weh (see *Prose Edda*, ch. 9), and with the generation of the kinds of humanity by Woden, or Ríg (see 'Rígsthula' in the *Poetic Edda*).

In the Troth, the gods Tiw and Woden are the gods of the sovereign powers of consciousness; Thunar is the god of physical force; and the Wanes, and especially Freya and Frey, are the divinities of generation.

Within society these forces must be developed, enhanced, and recognized for their true values and for how they relate to one another in a healthy world.

These same forces also should be recognized within each individual man and woman—each of us is to contain some of the sovereign-magician, some of the warrior, and some of the farmer, worker, or craftsman in us. Each individual is balanced in a way that places him or her in one or the other of these camps. Here is where the guidance of the gods and goddesses is vital.

In getting back in touch with these traditional and timeless values, the true man or woman will not only be bringing him- or herself back to a healthy and complete way of being, but will, in their own vital ways, be helping to bring the whole world back into balance with its own framework. This framework has been badly damaged by the centuries of Christianism, which has sought to rob humanity of its sense of spiritual sovereignty, physical power, and lust for living—qualities which Christianism demanded that we foreswear. In retaking them in a systematic way we most thoroughly defeat these restrictions on the battlefield of the human heart.

13

The Truth of the Gods

The gods and goddesses are real and their tales are
true; they exist in a realm beyond individual human beings
or groups of them. Our deeds can awaken them or send
them to sleep, but they exist as long as we exist. The gods
and their tales, or myths, are eternally true. They are just as
true today as they were a thousand or two thousand years
ago. As living beings, the gods and goddesses too undergo
some change and growth, although by our measurements
it is very slow. More commonly, it is our understanding of
them that changes, and so we need a steady kind of thought
to hold onto their truths.

Having lost trust in their gods, it is quite typical for
people to shift their understanding of them as beings moving on a lower plane of existence. This happened in the
ancient Greek and Roman religions when certain thinkers
began to spread the doctrine that the gods had really been
extraordinary men of the dim past who had, either by their
greatness or by their trickery, convinced the people that
they were gods (or when the historical understanding of
them promoted these gods to celestial stations). This may
seem convincing to some currently, because it seems more
"rational"; or it may be more attractive because the religion

now passing away, Christianity, puts so much emphasis on the existence of its god, Jesus, in human form. In any event, the belief that, for example, Woden was a chieftain-shaman of the dim past who led his tribe of Ases out of Asia and conquered the North, established himself as king and was eventually promoted to godhood, is very destructive to the living essence of the Troth.

First, such notions were originally generated in the classical world while faith in the gods of Greece and Rome was waning, which is a bad sign to begin with. Then it must be realized that Christian monks took up this theme as a form of anti-pagan propaganda, which went something like: "The old gods were evil human tricksters working against the people, and Christ came to save them from this trickery." In one fell swoop, the true gods were demonized, reduced in rank (to human), and made into isolated historical figures that could be written off as dead and gone. Of course, this propaganda only partially worked.

Some would like to claim that the gods and goddesses were both divinities *and* individual, historical humans. There are two problems with this: first, the gods *were* not, they *are* divinities. To simply relegate the gods to the past is to put them in a half-dead condition in our minds. The second problem is uniqueness. If Woden was a prehistoric king, then he, or some essential aspect of him, becomes isolated, trapped in a historical snare. Once a god has become a man, and that man dies, the relevance of that god eventually recedes into obscurity. The god becomes a prisoner of its unique manifestation. Witness what is happening to the Christ.

As a matter of fact the gods and goddesses can often, if only temporarily, become human. They can manifest in individual humans who are especially devoted to them, or who have certain runic techniques to become whole with the god for a specific purpose. But these are only partial phenomena, and the continuance of this is also dependent on realizing the timeless living nature of the gods and goddesses. For if the god is dead, how can it manifest in a follower?

What could possibly be gained by believing that the gods were once human? Nothing: for they would be dead. " ... Of what gain is a good man dead?" asks the *Edda* (Hávamál 71). It is most wise to know that the gods and goddesses are timeless living beings, as alive today as they were yesterday.

14

The Earth and the World

The most virulent and vicious propaganda that has been spread about the true character of our old heathenry is that it was a simple form of "nature worship." One look with an open eye at the mythology and the tales of our gods and goddesses will show that nothing could be further from the truth. In fact it is Christianity which is nothing but a misunderstood and disguised form of simple nature worship. Their charge of "nature worship" is a projection of their own fears concerning their actual natures. Unfortunately, the doctrines of materialistic scientism which followed those of Christianity in the recent past continued in this direction. Many early scholars of mythology, following a now-outdated evolutionary model, held that early man worshipped nature; then came "religion" (that is, Christianity), and finally science, which has come to save humanity from its various superstitions. In fact the materialistic rationalists were deluding themselves in the same way the Christians had earlier. These are the actual "nature worshippers"! Nature has but one law, the Christian god has but one law, "science" seeks to have but one law. The true spirit has manifold laws and ways, and this is reflected in the manifold ways of the Troth, both in nights of yore and now.

Nature is greatly revered and loved by those in the Troth, but it is loved for what it is and what it gives us, not for something that it is not. There was nature before there were the gods and goddesses, and there was nature before there were men and women. The gods of primeval consciousness, Woden, Willi and Weh, rebelled against the natural order, killed Ymir, and fashioned a new order of the cosmos based on their apprehension of a higher order of being. Forces of nature—etins, rises, and thurses—which are hostile to this consciousness-based order are trying, like the unthinking forces of nature that they are, to erode the divinely wrought strongholds of the spirit forged in Asgard and Midgard.

In Midgard itself, the *organic* vehicle of human life (symbolically shown to be *trees* in the mythology) existed before the gods of consciousness imparted their gifts and made humanity a spiritual creature akin to the gods. In all of this we see the point repeated that there is an organic, natural existence that is separate from the spiritual existence of the gods. The gods and goddesses need nature to fulfill their aims of expanding the empire of consciousness as widely and as deeply as possible—but the relationship of the gods, and hence of mankind, to nature is somewhat ambivalent. On the one hand, nature is a useful partner in attaining some aims; it is also the source of endless pleasure and in many ways the proving-ground for the gods (Midgard is the mirror of Asgard). The ultimate human pleasure is the holy harmony of body and soul, and this is only possible in the realm of Midgard. Through Midgard, and best through Midgard, can the gods truly fulfill themselves. However, forms of nature unallied with the gods pose the greatest threat to the noble aims of the divinities. All humans can directly feel this ambivalence toward nature in their own lives and experience.

The good and beneficial aspects of nature are reflected

in the Troth in the form of the good Earth, Midgard, and the wise and good etins, who have made alliances with the Ases and Wanes. Regardless of our alliance, the distinction remains between the Earth and the World. The Earth can be worshipped (as can many of the etins) as a beneficial manifestation of nature—this is a legitimate expression within the Troth as well. But the contrast between the Earth and the World is a stark one. The word "world" is really a combination of the words "wer(e)," which means "man" (as in "were-wolf"), and "old," which is an ancient noun for "age," or "aeon." So the "wer-old," the age of man, is really a term for the spiritual existence and experience of humanity, when contrasted with the physical or natural existence of the Earth. It is in the world that the gods exist, and it is in the world that humanity truly exists as well—at least that part of humanity that separates it from the animal and allies it with the gods. The Earth, as such, is seen as the most beautiful expression of Midgard, and this Earth is seen as almost purely good. The vast amount of ill that is present is the result of intrusions from Outgard.

So it can be seen that the work of the Troth is the work of the growth of the ways of the gods and goddesses, which is something quite different and apart from the "natural laws." If anything is worshipped in the Troth it is the ways of the gods and goddesses. These usually work in harmony and in tandem with the laws of nature, especially in the realm of the Wanes; but among the Ases, and especially with the god Woden, these ways may often seem very strange and non-natural indeed. The Troth teaches the rightness of the full spectrum of possibilities, and in so doing continues the work of the divine rebellion.

15

In Nights of Yore

Time is not what most of us have been taught it is. The Judeo-Christian religious notion of the linear, historical nature of time—that a god created the world out of nothing, that it is undergoing a linear progression (according to his "plan"), and will eventually end—has intruded on our own mythic senses from one side. At the same time the present capitalistic (some might call it "Protestant") work ethic has led to a similar perception of our own lives, and of our day-in, day-out existence. The model of time that people have, or the model of time foisted on them by others, has a "magical" effect. If you change the way you perceive time, on both a large and a small scale, you change the way you see the world, or "wer-old." The Christians hit upon this, perhaps unthinkingly, and it was their mission to cut the folk off from its past, and to hurl the folk into a "future."

Time is not really a straight line. In fact, it cannot be reduced to any one way of thinking about it. Time can be, and is constantly, subject to the moldings and reshapings of our minds. We experience this every day: as things bore us, time seems to drag; when we are enjoying ourselves, time flies.

In the Troth, time is molded in many ways. In chapter 9 we saw how the year is shaped according to the cycles of nature. Cyclical time is important to the workings of the powers of generation and regeneration. Time eternally returns to itself. What is done in those holy points of return is a matter in the hands of the true. If right blessings are done, if the right gifts are given, the cycles of eternal return hold or seek the best level of beings and well-being.

The timeless ring of tides is not the only way of working with time. Our very tongue shows us that the ancient Teutonic time conception was one that acknowledged the independent reality of only two "times," the Past and the Present (or Non-Past), or the "then" and "now." This is shown by the fact that we have only a present-tense "I am" and a past-tense "I was." If we want to form the future we have to bring in a "helping" verb (which is also in the present)—"I will be." This is not theoretical claptrap, but clear and everyday reality. It, like the fact that we constantly invoke the gods and goddesses of our folk in the week-day names, is just hidden by the very *familiarity* of the thing.

In this understanding of times there is a Past, which is known and *real*. In it are the eternally true myths and old saws of the folk, as well as the precedents of law, and other matters of eternally true lore. The great Then is a vast field of meaning and being, complex and deep. The Now is the thin edge of a sword blade, always now and unendingly narrow; the force and weight behind it is the great Then as it cuts through the even-greater sea of the unknown stretching out before us. This is really a more *realistic* view of time and human experience. It is also one that gives us hope and meaning based on our eternally true past, into which we enter at the tides of blessing and there feed on the truth of the nights of yore. The workings of the blessings and sumbles, of the hearing and telling of the tales of our gods and heroes, all work to ensure the right kind of "future" and to make it less fluid. If we always link ourselves to the greatest deeds and doings of our gods and goddesses, of our heroic ancestors, we will become more and more like them, and thereby be able to meet whatever is coming in the best possible way.

Now we could ask ourselves, what is the nature of this "then" in the past/non-past model? Clearly, it is not the "past" as understood by the Judeo-Christian (or Marxist) linear scheme. In that scheme the past is seen as an objective string of isolated events, lives and actions, which only find their reality as they are directed from the outside—by god's plan, by a historical dialectic, etc. That is, there is thought to be *real history*, which is seen as an unfolding (not a true evolution) of a pre-conceived pattern moving from one static point in time to another.

Time is always subject to our manipulations. This is true of the present and it is twice as true of the past. We all manipulate in an unthinking manner—we remember what we *want* to remember. So the Then is not really a collection of random, isolated actions, but rather an inner mental pattern which has been shaped by the soul. Individuals remember past events only in accordance with their pre-existing mental patterns, and so it is with whole cultures. Only recently has the academic discipline of history come to the realization that its picture is the result of an endless complex of refinements, reductions, interpretations, willful distortions, and re-shaping of any meager "facts" which might have been at the historians' disposal. Thus, knowledge about what really happened, even for the most "recent" past, is hardly obtainable.

So what are we left with? Only everything that is important, relevant, and absolutely necessary. We see that with the true pattern of time, the great Then takes on a higher shaping function which ensures a continuing dynamic evolution—an unending growth through the cycles of existence. Stasis, or standing still, is not its aim, but rather dynamism: fluctuating movement. Flux and movement are the surest signs of life. Flux is life, stability is death.

"Pastness" is the stuff of our myths and legends. It is that which is always worth remembering, because it is always true. The words of the *Edda* are no less meaningful today than they were a thousand years ago. The myths are really not quaint anecdotes from the past, but rather eternally true *ideals* which we are striving to impose (by force of will) upon the "future." This is done in the working of the blessings and sumbles. In the sumble, for example, the participants gather, arrange themselves in a certain order symbolic of their orderings within the society present, and drink an intoxicating brew while reciting oaths, boasts, and most especially mythic deeds of the gods and ancestors. When the gathered folk enter into this rite, they symbolically enter into the great Then inhabited by the gods and heroes. They harmonize with, and then begin to assimilate, the very being of the great Then. At the conclusion of the sumble, the gathered folk return to the ordinary world of the Now—but they are changed, somehow strengthened by their contact with the holy world of the gods. Armed with what they have brought back from the great Then, they are ready to sail forth across the great sea of the unknown.

16

The Edge of the Sword

To the outsider what is done in the Troth may very often seem like a sort of "worshipping of the past." This is accurate only in so far as the true meaning of the previous chapter has been understood. People who are in close contact with what is *essentially* and *eternally* true about themselves are actually those who are most able not only to cope with the ever-changing, ever-challenging onrush of the great unknown sea of the future, but who are most likely to be able to *master* it. Again, we could invoke the modern example of the Japanese, who have in the past hundred years or so gone from a feudal state to an ultramodern/high-tech society without giving up their abiding folk-values. In fact, it is precisely those values which have enabled them to make this transition.

The traditional *use* of the great idealized *Then* is in the most effective "conquest" of the great hypothetical sea of the future. The sword's edge is always turned forward. So, paradoxically perhaps, in ritually focusing periodically on the *Then*, we are actually enabling ourselves to most powerfully focus on our being in the ever-present Now and are thus able to shape that which is to come. Some segments of the neo-Teutonic movement seem to be running from the present, and trying to take refuge in the past. This is an essential betrayal of the spirit of the forebears. The great *Then* is there to strengthen our hands and sharpen our blades, to help us to be here in the *Now*, and to enable us to go forward with good speed. Those who fear the present, those who quake before the sea of the great unknown, those who seek to flee into the past to find comfort there, do so because they are out of touch with the truths bound up in the nights of yore. Those whose hearts have been strengthened by the truth of the elder lore will be known by their deeds. They, like the forebears, will not fear that which is coming, but will have the inner weapons to win the day and sail on into the night.

17

The Soul

Athem they had not,
being nor bearing,
athem gave Woden,
being, Lodhurr,

wode they had not,
nor blooming hue;
Hœnir gave wode,
and blooming hue.
(Völuspá 18)

In the middle of everything is the human soul, by which we gauge the world and the Earth and see them for ourselves. No other area of knowledge has been so wracked by the ravages of the forces of Christianity than our own native "psychology" or, simply put, "teachings about the soul." If a people knows something well and in intimate detail, its language will usually have many words for that thing expressing all its nuances and variations. It is sometimes said that the Eskimos have so many words for snow and for the color white because they know these so well and are used to making fine distinctions among and between the varieties of these things. In ancient-times the Teutonic peoples had a bewildering number of names for the "soul," "spirit," "mind," and so forth. This is telling in two ways: it shows an intimate knowledge of the thing and it shows a "technical" knowledge which does not refer to a dogma or psychological school of any kind. It was a deep understanding implicit in the very language.

To recover the lost understandings of the Teutonic

soul and its workings would be the single greatest key to
once and for all re-quickening the withered roots of the
Troth. It is probably no accident that serious work in the
investigation of the nature of the human soul, divorced
from the superstitious dogmas of the Christians, and the
revival of the knowledge of the god of the soul, Woden,
began at the same time. Despite the many wrong turns and
dead ends of the often-misguided investigators, there has
been progress. Perhaps no other school of modern psychological teaching has been more beneficial than that
founded by the Swiss psychiatrist Carl Jung.

But what we present here is an attempt to recover the
old traditional lore of the soul as it was understood by our
ancestors. Here we will also reconstruct, for modern use, a
practical native terminology for talking about the "souls."
The first step in doing so is the realization that there is not
one "soul," but many, and that there is no one word, other
than perhaps "self," that encompasses all aspects of the
many "souls." The self stands at the center of the souls and
can be the stead where all are held together. This is not,
however, a natural phenomena, but rather something for
which a man or woman must work. Also, it must be realized
that the strong body-soul split so heavily emphasized in
Christianity is missing in true soul-lore. We would rather
talk of a body-soul-mind complex for a more complete
understanding not only of what the parts are, but also how
they relate to one another.

Figure 17.1 sums up much of the image of the human
soul in the traditional sense, although it is not exhaustive.
In explaining this diagram, we will start with the center,
and with the most familiar, and work our way out.

In the very middle we see the self. It is, in its own way,
among the most mysterious aspects, and the least familiar
one to the everyday experience of many, because it is deep
within—behind the eye of our soul, as it were. It grows and

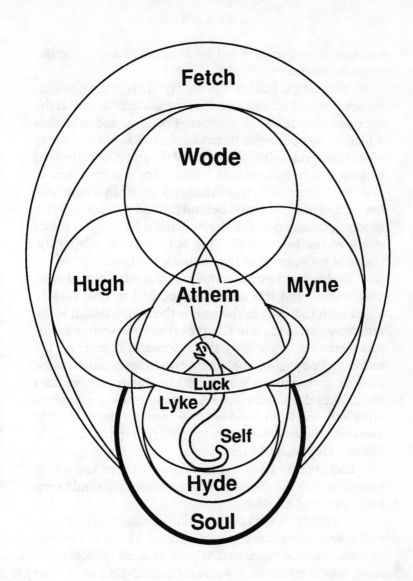

Figure 17.1: The Image of the Soul

91

becomes strong as it is fed by true deeds and profound inner experience.

The *lyke* (or *lich*) is the "body." This is the physical vehicle with which most parts of the soul are fused. It is the doorway through which experience is gained and that which allows our wills to have effect. It is not, as others would have you think, an enemy of the spirit, but is indeed its best friend in the whole scheme. For it allows man to exist in Midgard—his true home and the stead where he is best suited to do his work. Behind the body is a sort of mysterious, plasmic quasi-material usually having the rough shape of the body itself. This can be called simply the shape or form, or more traditionally the *hyde*.

The *hugh* is the intellectual and analytical part of man. The "mind" and the will are embodied in this. Closely allied with this part of the soul is the *myne*, which is the reflective part of the mind. In the *myne* is the well of ancestral memories, as well as those personal ones from the individual's own lifetime. These two aspects should work in close harmony with one another. The myne provides material of deep and eternal significance for the hugh to work on, and both working together can come to right answers. These soul-aspects are reflected in the ravens of Woden: Huginn and Muninn.

The breath of life is the *athem*. It keeps the whole being fed with the energies that sustain it in life and "keep body and soul together."

The other aspects of the "soul" are more mysterious, and are not often directly experienced. This is in contrast to those already discussed which, at least on some low level, we experience every waking moment of the day and through the dreams of sleep.

Wode is the new English form that we would have for that essential aspect of Wod-en—the power of "inspiration" or even "mania," as the Greeks would have called it.

Experience of this is extraordinary; it constitutes an "altered state of consciousness."

The *fetch* can be understood in the traditional sense of an entity separate from the individual, but which is attached to him/her for the duration of his/her life. It is the conduit through which the gods communicate to him/her, and the embodiment of all that he/she has ever been. It is a storehouse of images and powers from beyond this life and from beyond Midgard. It stores up all the experiences of this life in order that it can go on beyond this life to continue its work. The fetch is very rarely experienced in any direct way. For most it only "appears" when death is near, when a man is "fay." The fetch is that which is responsible for the common phenomenon of one's life "passing before one's eyes" just before death, or the appearances of spectral female figures at that time. The fetch is seen as an entity of the sex opposite that of the person in question. Closely associated with the fetch is the luck of a person. It can also have a guardian aspect, in which case it can be called the warden. In it is housed all of the echoes of all of the deeds ever done by the bodies to which the fetch has ever been bound. This will be discussed further in the next two chapters. The soul is, in the technical sense, the psychic body, or "shade," which embodies the self after the death of the lyke.

This knowledge about the traditional nature of the human being in all essential aspects, and the teachings of rebirth and of wyrd bound up with it, can have the results most true men and women desire. However, those who wish to delve deeper into these realms will have to take up the lore of the runes.

18

Rebirth

*"Hinder her not   Helward to fare,
whence back never   she be born again!"*
(Short Lay of Sigurth 45)

Many modern commentators upon the ancient troth would have us believe that your forebears held extremely confused ideas concerning the destiny of the human soul after death. This was never the case! Although our true forefathers were never bound by a rigid dogma, they formulated a lore based on direct experience, astute observation of nature, and intuitive wisdom. The form of the lore which they developed was rather complex, but no more complex than the manifold world and the human soul reflected in it. This elegant complexity baffled the simple-minded monks, and even most later nineteenth-century scholars. It seemed to them that our heathen ancestors possessed only a confused mass of mutually contradictory conceptions. It never occurred to them that all these ideas could have been held at the same time by minds firmly rooted in self-knowledge and standing tall in Midgard.

The "soul" is made up of several entities, each with its own special work to do (see chapter 17). Some may find it more convenient at this time to consider these aspects as "levels of consciousness," or as "states of being." Although certain aspects, such as the hugh and the hyde, are important for some matters having to do with the fate of the human soul after death, it is the fetch which is more important to the process of rebirth, or "reincarnation." The fetch can be passed from one person to another after death, just as luck can be passed in part or as a whole from one living person to another. The travels of this fetch-being really outline what we mean by traditional and true "reincarnation" or rebirth.

The various soul aspects are thought to have a variety of destinations after death. The hugh may go to Valhalla or to Hel or to some other godly abode. The hyde will remain with the lyke in the burial mound or, if the body is burned, both will be destroyed, thus leaving the hugh and other aspects unbound. In ancient times it was thought that the hyde still connected to the lyke was responsible for such phenomena as the "walking dead." The fetch and luck bound together would, if nature were allowed to take her course, be reborn within the clan or tribe from generation to generation. The recently dead ancestors were thought to be actually reborn in the newly born descendants. These diverse beliefs did not come into conflict with one another due to the special way in which the human soul and the world were understood. The multiplicity of souls and the variety of functions and destinations of these entities after death were concepts which were vigorously attacked by the forces of Christianity, and are therefore concepts which must be vigorously pursued and renewed by the true folk.

At this point it must be stressed that in ancient times it was not believed that the personal consciousness, with memories intact, was reincarnated—only certain innate transpersonal powers and characteristics as well as certain obligations and weaknesses were. Also, it was not the free-form, arbitrary parlor-room version of "reincarnation" where souls go flying off to distant parts of the globe to be reborn as Chinese or Polynesians. Rebirth only naturally comes about through a direct contact between the one losing the fetch and the one gaining her. This contact may be genetic, or it may be physical. A powerful act of will can also cause such a transference.

In the normal course of events, the fetch departs the dying man and remains in Hel (the abode of the dead) until someone in the clan (that is, someone of close genetic relationship to the dead man) gives birth. The fetch then returns and begins to reattach itself to this newborn baby during the first nine nights of the baby's life. The naming rite in which the child is taken into the stream of life and into the family tradition is the final phase of this reintegration. This may, if you will, be understood as a mythic or ritualized explanation of "genetics," but in the lore of the ancestors it was much more.

The name rightly given to a child is that of a recently dead (or long-dead) ancestor. This name is chosen either because the ancestor appears to the mother, father, or elder in a dream during the time of pregnancy, or because it is simply "known" what name should be given to the child. The child will then be held to *be* the ancestor reborn into the family, that is, the namesake is the bearer of the innate powers, abilities, and obligations of the forebear. But the newborn possesses a unique and original hugh and athem. Thus there is an interweaving of the transpersonal blood-line with a singular individual unique in all the world. It is now the task of this new individual, who is a perfect blend of the powers and obligations of the past and the hopes and responsibilities of what is to come, to go forth, and by deeds of honor add to the forces of luck and power in the family and clan. Thus the whole of the clan and of the folk is seen to be made up of both the living and the dead. It may be viewed as a family tree, with the ancestral roots providing the continuing nourishment from the realm of the dead and the branches giving unending energy from the realm of the living.

This whole body of lore probably goes back to Indo-European times. Actually, similar beliefs are known to have been held by the Greeks, Celts, and Thracians. The Vedic Indian form of "reincarnation" was also originally identical to the one outlined here. Only later did it degenerate into a "moral system."

The true man or woman desires above all things rebirth in Midgard. Because this is the realm most right for us, this is the true realm where our work is to be wrought. For many who cannot go on, and who become weary of soul, the eternal rest of Hel will come; while for others who are called to a higher duty the halls of Woden or Freya beckon. For many of the noble and true souls of Midgard rebirth in human flesh in this world is the highest good. The Eddics quote at the beginning of this chapter is a curse formula spoken over Brynhild by Hogni, who is wishing her ill by wishing that she not be reborn in this world.

It should be fairly clear that this form of belief is far and away better than the "otherworldly-ness" of Christianity, which is certainly based on a manipulative propaganda ploy. The former is the metaphysic that makes what was said in chapter 10 complete and whole. It is practical and rather "hard-headed" as such religious doctrines go, but it has the intuitive ring of authenticity that is spellbinding. This process goes on whether we believe in it or not. It can be traced and investigated through history and folklore. But as a practical system for the understanding and transformation of the individual and the world, it will work much better once its principles are again grasped and used.

In everyday practical religious work it can be seen why it is so important to name children in traditional ways and by following the ritual given by our lore. Parents who cut off the child from its spiritual heritage could be cutting it off from a whole set of powers and abilities as well.

19

Wyrd

It is many times said of the Teutonic peoples that they were and are a "fatalistic" lot. Much is generally made of "fatalism" in the religion, especially when it comes to leading a heroic life. Since now more than ever we need heroes, this becomes a very important point for the full understanding of the Troth as it is to be lived today. There is, however, a great deal of misconception surrounding what is truly meant by the notion of "fate."

Usually when we hear the word "fate," which is of Latin and not Teutonic origin, we think of ideas such as predestination. That is, it is usually loaded with the idea that "fate" is something that a *transcendental* force (or god) has already pre-determined will happen to a person or group of persons. But this is not the usual concept in the Troth. Two words that indicate what "fate" really is to the Teutonic mind are *wyrd* (usual modern spelling "weird") and *ordeal*.

An or-deal was originally the result of action "dealt out" at some primeval stage. The "or-" means essentially the "primordial, oldest, or outermost" of the concept indicated by the stem word. Thus "fate" is the result of actions which the person—or his fetch!—performed at some previous time. These actions are the "dealing out" of what will follow in time. This is virtually identical to the Indian concept of *karma*, which also literally just means "action" (with the implication of reciprocal "re-action"). An Old Norse word containing the same concept is *ørlög*, which literally means "primal layers or laws." This indicates that the actions "laid down" in the past will continue to affect phenomena in the days and nights to come. This whole concept explains the metaphysic behind the old Teutonic practice of trial by ordeal—it was a magical manifestation of justice based on past action.

The word "wyrd" contains a similar quality. It is a noun developed from the Old English verb *weorthan*, to become or to turn. Thus wyrd is really that which has become (those "deals" already dealt out), that which affects the present, and that which is to come. The Old Norse form of this is *urdhr*, which is also the name of the first Norn. When something happens that has the eerie quality of having its roots in the eldrich past we properly call it "weird." (The word is, however, now misused to such an extent that it has lost most of its holy connotations.)

All of this explains the metaphysic behind the whole Teutonic system of law, best exemplified by English Common Law, based upon precedents (past layers of action) which determine what actions should be taken in the present and future. This is in sharp contrast to the Judeo-Roman form of law based on the decree of a transcendental force—a god or king. More and more, this latter situation is one in which we find ourselves today.

So far it is obvious that the Teutonic concept of "fate" (wyrd) is closely connected with concepts of time and causality. That which has become, the past, conditions the present and thus that which is to come. This, as so much else in the Troth, is a common-sense approach to the matter. The mystery of the Three Norns (or "Wyrd Sisters") gives us further keys to the understanding of wyrd. The names of the Norns in Old Norse are Urdhr ("that which has become"), Verdhandi ("that which is becoming"), and Skuld ("that which should or ought [to become]"). The first two *condition*, but do not *determine* the third. These conditions are produced by the deeds of the person who receives the fruits of those deeds. The Norns are not causal agents, but rather the numinous organisms through which the energies of actions are received, transformed, and re-directed back to their source.

Within the body-mind complex of the individual (see chapter 17) this works through the fetch. This aspect of the soul is attached to an individual and receives the energies of the actions of the individual and of those performed in the environment of the individual; it formulates these actions into a form which can be recirculated back into the life of the individual. There they will eventually have their effect. This is a totally amoral process, and purely organic in structure. This fetch is (or can be) passed from one life to the next along family lines, or is sometimes magically transferred free from clanic restrictions. In either case the accumulated past action (ordeal/wyrd) is passed from one life to another. It is clear that the old Teutonic concept of "fate" is in no way similar to the Christian concept of predestination. The true men and women of days of yore were at least able to know that they shaped their own destinies as a result of their own past actions. It is, however, easy to see how phenomena are misinterpreted as "fated," and thus beyond our control, when the events conditioning these phenomena are lost in the dim past (personal or transpersonal).

The true man or woman may want to investigate his or her wyrd, and this can be done in three realms of past action: 1) personal, 2) clanic, and 3) transpersonal. The first is past action contained within the parameters of the present life-time, while the latter two may be roughly considered as "past lives," one genealogically determined and the other from outside the clan. The first can be investigated through a personal retrospective of past deeds and events in one's life. The clanic realm is investigated through genealogical history, which in older times was considered an important source of spiritual knowledge. The knowledge of the transpersonal is drawn from the great storehouse of cosmic memories housed in the myne (or as the Jungians would call it, the "collective unconscious"). Contacts gained through connection with this aspect of the soul should not be understood as a "reincarnation" of the individuality. Knowledge from this realm may be gained through reflective techniques. This reflection is best undertaken under self-guidance, or with the help of trusted and true friends, as variations on this technique are rampant among storefront occultists, and it is often dressed up in the most shoddy, trite, and madcap cosmologies.

The concept of wyrd and ordeal play a central role in the religious world-view within the Troth. One of the greatest messages of the Troth to the individual is that he or she should "find destiny and follow it." There is a personal task and ordeal for all who would be true. The work of finding it is the work of finding the personal wyrd. This must, however, be approached in the old way of the North, free from Judeo-Christian notions of predestination and transcendental fatalism. The true man or woman is not manipulated by "fate," but is rather responsible for his or her own ordeal!

20

Runestaves

In nights of yore, when our elder troth was fading, one of the cultural features that was slowly eroded was the use of runes as a way of writing. Originally this was a system used mainly by magicians and within the cult of Woden. But later, and especially after Christianity and the culture of the South had made inroads into the Northern world, the runestaves were used more and more for normal, natural communication. Today the runes are being revived as a magical system, and as a system of initiation and self-development. For this the elder futhark system of twenty-four runes is normally used. However, as a work of the Troth it is vital that the knowledge of the runes be spread again among those who are drawn to them. Not all who learn of the runes today will want to use them in work of galdor or seith; that is really in the realm of the Rune-Gild. But as a way to revive the intellectual traditions of our folk, knowledge of the runes, and the promotion of them in religious contexts, can be a great boon.

The question then arises, *what* runic system should be used for this purpose. The answer is really quite simple. As we are using English, we should use the runic system designed for and by the folk speaking that tongue. This keeps the magical tradition, using the twenty-four runes, separate from the everyday system, which will make use of the thirty-three runes of the English manuscript tradition.

Using the table presented below, the reader will be able to write anything in modern English in runes—and have a real tradition behind him/her. Some slight modifications have had to be made to the Old English tradition, but they are in keeping with traditional guidelines. For those interested in the ancient and/or magical traditions, books in the bibliography will point you in the right direction. The table is presented in the traditional futhork order, as this is part of the intellectual heritage that the runes are intended to preserve. Every runestave has a special name which is a real word in natural language. It has symbolic meanings, which we do not have the space to go into here. We have given the New English equivalents of these names, and they should be used as the names of the "letters" when spelling something.

f	ᚠ	Fee
u	ᚢ	Urus (= aurochs)
th	ᚦ	Thorn
o	ᚩ	Ose (= the god = Woden) [short o]
r	ᚱ	Ride
ch	ᚳ	Char (= something burnt)

g/j	X	Gibbet (= a gallows)
w	ᛈ	Wyn (= joy)
h	ᚻ	Hail
n	ᚾ	Need
i	ǀ	Ice
y	ᛞ	Year
y	ᛄ	Yew (rarely used)
p	ᛈ	Perth (= a lot cup)
x	ᛉ	Elks
s	ᛋ	Sun
t	↑	Tiw (= the god's name)
b	ᛒ	Birch
e	ᛖ	Eean (= a year-old horse)
m	ᛗ	Man
l	ᛚ	Lake

ng	⊗	Ing (= the god Ing/Yngvi/Frey)
d	ᛞ	Day
o	ᛟ	Odal [long o]
oa	ᚩ	Oak
a	ᚪ	Ash
y	ᚣ	Yielding
ea	ᛠ	Earth
eo	ᛇ	Yeowell (= wheel of the year)
q(u)	ᛢ	Quern (= grain mill)
c/k	ᛣ	Cup (hard c or k)
st	ᛥ	Stone
g	⊗	Gar (=spear)

It will be noticed that there are more runes than there are letters in our alphabet. To write them properly, one must pay attention to whether, for example, one is writing a "g" as in "get" [⊗, gar], or the "g" as in "giant" [ᚷ,

gibbet]. Also, certain runestaves can serve for two Roman letters. Note: ᚦ = th, ᚺ =ch, ᚼ = ng, ᛗ = st ᛦ = ea.

All in all, spelling in runes can be a matter of individual inspiration and creativity. It should never be bound by the same kind of rules that bind modern English spelling in Roman letters. If ever in doubt, use phonetics as your best guide.

The punctuation used when writing in these modern runes is as follows: All words are divided one from the other by a single dot [·], commas are a double dot [:], and periods are a triple dot [⫶].

ᚦᚢᛋ·ᚠᚨᚪᚦᛝ·ᚦᚠᛏ·ᛚᚨᛏ·ᛒᛗ·ᚹᚱᛁᛏᛏᛖᚨ·
ᛁᚨ·ᚱᛟᛗᚨᚾ·ᛚᛖᛏᛏᛖᚱᛋ·ᚺᚨᚾ·ᛒᛖ·ᛏᛋᛁᛚ
ᚪ·ᚱᛖᚾᚻᛖᚱᛖᚻ·ᛁᚾ·ᚱᚢᚾᛖᛋ⫶

21

Holy Tokens

Like all religions, the Troth is rich in holy signs and symbols. In fact, many of the sacred symbols of Christianity were in some measure taken from the older traditions of the Troth and our kindred faiths in the Indo-European stream. In the second part of this book you will see described many tokens (signs) of holy meaning, some as gestures (such as the "hammer-sign"), others as natural objects (such as the horn, harrow, and so forth). They will each be described in their place.

What we want to turn our minds to here are the holy signs that may seem mysterious (such as the Knot of the Slain) or carry historical misconceptions, (such as the sun-wheel or Thunar's hammer). These should be explained so that the individual true man or woman will be able to use and interpret the various signs and symbols held to be holy by the Troth.

The Knot of the Slain (Old Norse: *valknutr*; illustrated at right) has several variant forms. Generally it appears to be three triangles linked together (3 x 3 = 9), or three interlocked drinking horns. The Knot of the Slain is the official sign of the Rune-Gild and of the way of Woden. It symbolizes the power of Woden to bind and unbind the soul.

The Hammer of Thunar (left) has many shapes and variations. At the time when Christianity was making strong headway in the North, it became the fashion for those true to their own gods to take the Hammers of Thunar, which many carried as concealed amulets, out of hiding to wear proudly as a sign of their troth. The reappearance of the hammer in these times is a sign of the re-emergence of the Troth. Therefore, all who are true should have and wear a hammer. The Hammer of Thunar is that weapon with which he wards the realm of the gods and goddesses, and with which he pushes back the realm of the thurses, making way for the light of the Ases and Wanes.

The Sun-Wheel was, of course, used by the National Socialist movement in Germany, and has thus become attached to that movement in most people's minds. We cannot, however, allow historical events to de-termine what holy signs we can or cannot use. The Sun-Wheel was holy before the Nazis used it, and it continues to be as holy today. Its symbolism is shared with the Hammer of Thunar (which it is also sometimes called), but it goes beyond that meaning into the realm of general cosmic dynamism and eternal return. It is the sign of the eternal cycle, wielded for the good of the true.

The Troth-Rune (right) is the official sign of the Ring of Troth. It is a bind-rune made up of the Ring of Troth and embodies the yew-rune of eternal life and death, the wynn-rune, which binds all siblings together in troth as inspired by the gods (ᚹ), and the need-rune, show-ing that we are returning out of need to the way of our fore-bears.

The Yrminsul (right) is the sign of the axis of the world. It is a symbol of the northward orien-tation of our attention, as it has its apex at the Northern Star. Further, it is a symbol of cosmic order, as defined by the god Tiw, of whose rune the Yrminsul is also a sign.

Freya's Heart (left) is the sign of the blessings of the goddess Freya, and is the symbol of those given to her mysteries. This was only later "reinterpreted" as a "heart," as it may in fact be an iconic sign of the female mons and buttocks. This "reinterpretation" saved it from the same fate of many of the rest of Freya's mysteries so hated by the Christians.

These are only a few of the many tokens and signs held to be holy in the Troth. Each god and goddess has signs sacred to him or her. But above and beyond them all at this time is the Hammer of Thunar. It is the token most sacred at this point because it expresses our dynamic and energetic growth, as well as our determination to defend and expand our heritage.

22

The Right Ways

The Troth teaches the Nine Noble Virtues and the Six-fold Goal as being the right ways to form the everyday deeds and doings of true men and women in Midgard. Our highest duties remain in the trust of and togetherness with the gods and goddesses of the folk, and in the continuance of that folk in which they live. These high tasks may seem somewhat vague and indefinite, but they are quickened and given shape by the Nine Noble Virtues and the Six-fold Goal.

In chapter 2 we saw how the Troth may be approached from within the self, and how one can find the right roads to travel in seeking and finding the Troth and what is true. The inner road is one every true man and woman must travel, and travel alone, to come to the truth of his or her own heart. The Troth does, however, also have a general set of *ethical* guidelines to help steer the ship of the self on its right and true course. These guidelines are especially needed when looking at the possibilities of a true land in the years to come.

The Six-Fold Goal

To have a true set of ethics a clear set of goals or aims must be laid out. If someone is asked or even ordered to do something, he or she will want to know that this request is given in order to attain some greater end to which he or she also aspires. We can all see how demoralizing it is when, for example, soldiers are told to put their lives on the line for reasons not fully understood by those who order them to do so. When the aim of the mission is lost, the ship will soon lose its course, and the very fiber of the ship and its crew will become rotten. After describing a set of goals, the details of true ethics can for the most part be derived from them. The day-in, day-out dedication to the principles of the Sixfold Goal is the greatest power available to true men and women in the restoration of our holy way. In the years to come, if we are to gain and grow, and be able to hold and harness that which we have built, a true set of ethics drawn from a set of high goals must be established.

The Sixfold Goal is something hidden deep within the folk. It was there in the days and nights of yore, and it remains in us today. Some parts of it can only be glimpsed here and there; other parts can be seen shining constantly through everything we do as a culture. The burden of the foreign, Eastern cult of Christianity has obscured, usurped and twisted some of the Goals, and repressed their soul. The piecemeal approach that has been available to us for some centuries has been a slow one. Here we regain parts of our system of laws, there we regain the freedom to buy and sell as we will, over there we regain some of our freedom to love as we will, while here we awaken to a sense of the joy of conquest; but somehow the freedoms we are striving toward seem not to have the rewards we expected. The reason for this is that the soul of what we are striving after is missing. That which holds it all together, a true set of goals and a truly reborn world, has been missing. The missing key lies in the fact that all of these deep-level urges are really parts of a greater whole, and that all parts of the whole must be seen and developed in order for any part of it to be truly successful.

The Sixfold Goal is a deep-level gift of the gods and goddesses, and is a reflection of their qualities in us and in our world, or society. These are the true goals of true men and women living together in harmony and peace, protected and expanded by the might of arms, ruled over by wisdom and justice. In a traditional pattern, the Sixfold Goal may be shown thus:

1. RIGHT   2. WISDOM
3. MIGHT
4. HARVEST   5. FRITH
6. LOVE

These six goals are the worthy things of the world, the things worth dying for, the things we must hold dear. We must not only defend what remains of them, but expand them forever into constant fulfillment. On the most practical level, if someone asks a true man or woman "what they stand for," it is the holding and hoisting of the Sixfold Goal that should be his or her answer.

RIGHT is ruled over by Tiw. It is the justice of law shaped by the lore of our folk and meted out with good judgment and true by those who can see the truth. This is a goal rationally sought and rationally administered—the rule of rationality and enlightenment in the world. From this our desire to see a world ruled rationally is derived.

WISDOM is watched over by Woden. This is the hidden lore and powers welling up from the darkest depths of our souls and hovering high over our heads, shining beyond the clouds, and leading us on into the unknown. This is the mysterious force that has the ability to hold all things together, ruled by those who can see and understand the whole. Above all, wisdom must be preserved, for in it are the wells of all memory; if it and only it survives, all other parts of the whole may be regenerated. From this is derived our sense of adventure, our curiosity about the unknown, our seeking and questing character.

MIGHT is wielded by Thunar. In might is embodied the twofold goal of victory and defense, which both depend on pure power or might for their ultimate right. Without this pivotal goal, all others will fall into decay and be overcome by things outside the truth—as indeed they have been. But might must be ruled over by right and wisdom, and must serve the purposes of harvest and frith. There is worth in might in and of itself, however. In the bodily expression of power is found the joy of victory which acts as a balm on the soul of the warrior. The goal of conquest and exercise of might can be turned without or within the true man or woman—but it must find expression. From this is derived our hunger for conquests, big and small, and our great will to power.

HARVEST is holy to the Wanes. This is the reaping of the things of the good cycles of nature, which ensures that the folk continues to flourish in the world, that the livestock abound in good health, and that the seed is rightly planted, cut, and threshed. Harvest is the overriding need for organic continuance—for the continuance of organic life. Harvest here includes all of the fruits of economic cycles. It is the goodness of plenty, of wealth, and physical well-being. Today our society and our desire for abundance and wealth is dominated by this value system.

FRITH is ruled by Frey and Freya. Frith is our own word for "peace." Frith is the true state of "peace" wherein all parts of the Sixfold Goal are successfully pursued and attained by a society. In frith is true freedom, for frith is the essence of freedom, the state in which self-directed, self-willed growth and development can take place. Frith usually implies an absence of war but not of struggle or conflict, which must always be present on some level when true growth is taking place. In frith we do not stand still; in frith we learn how to take our fights to ever higher fields. Right/might/frith form a powerful axis. Might provides the protection frith needs to promote freedom, but might must be ruled by right to protect frith in turn from ungoverned might. From frith comes our almost universal desire for "peace," but if we misunderstand what this means, we can bring ourselves not "peace" but stagnation and death.

LOVE is the law of life and is embodied in Frey and Freya, the "Lord and Lady." This is the pure powerful love, or the "lust" of eroticism. In it is our sense of play and pure pleasure. The stem word from which "love" is derived really has to do with the enjoyment of (physical) pleasure. That we all seek this as a goal in itself is natural and good, but it is not without its non-natural or "spiritual" sides, to be sure. In seeking pleasure we show and more importantly *experience* an unbridled lust for life itself. This deep well of desire acts from below much the way wisdom does from above; in fact there is a secret bond between them. Wisdom and love hold the six goals together. Among the six goals, this is the one most hated by the Christian forces. Its revenge shall be sweet.

Thinking about these six goals as the things always worth striving for (as far as the whole of the Troth and its folk are concerned, as well as for individual true men and women in their own lives), will act as a guidepost for holding true values. These goals were sometimes unspoken, but always implicit in all that was done in nights of yore.

Nine Noble Virtues

Beyond these goals, which will form the direction of one's ethical actions, there are the Nine Noble Virtues. These have been a part of the whole revival movement in the Anglo-American world, and they act as handy reminders of the day-in, day-out values of our folk. But even they are in the end somewhat pointless without knowledge of the six goals. The Nine Noble Virtues are:

1. Courage (heartiness)
2. Truth
3. Honor (worthiness)
4. Fidelity (troth)
5. Discipline (hardiness)
6. Hospitality (friendliness)
7. Industriousness (work)
8. Self-reliance (freedom)
9. Perseverance (steadfastness)

Courage is the bravery to do what is right at all times. Truth is the willingness to be honest and say what one knows to be true and right. Honor is the feeling of inner value and worth from which one knows that one is noble of being, and the desire to show respect for this quality when it is found in the world. Fidelity is the will to be loyal to one's gods and goddesses, to one's folk, and to one's self. Discipline is the willingness to be hard with one's self first, and then if need be with others, in order that greater purposes can be achieved. Hospitality is the willingness to share what one has with one's fellows, especially when they are far from home. Industriousness is the willingness to work hard—always striving for efficiency—as a joyous activity in itself. Self-reliance is the spirit of independence which is achieved not only for the individual but also for the family, clan, tribe, and nation. Perseverance is that spirit of stick-to-it-iveness that can always bring one back from defeat or failure—each time we fail we recognize failure for what it is and, if the purpose is true and good, we persevere until success is won.

All true men and women strive to keep holy the Nine Noble Virtues. How each of these is to be understood is largely a matter of personal thought and family values. In a more traditional world, these Nine Noble Virtues might be spoken to us by our kindly elders as: "Be hearty, forthright, worthy, true, hard, friendly, hard-working, free and stead-fast in all that you undertake." If these values are taught and held by ourselves for ourselves and for our offspring, a solid groundwork will be laid for the rebirth of the Troth. All of these values, not just some of them, must be prac-ticed and taught as the Nine Noble Virtues. Too often these values have been passed on under false guises, such as the so-called "Protestant work ethic," and in other such non-sense. These are *our* values, made for us and by us, and have nothing whatsoever to do with the foreign cult.

23

Into the Unknown

From our own lives, and from what has been said of the lore of time and how it works, we know that the "future" is unknown and unknowable with any certainty. To be sure, the wyrd of our folk is laid, and our ordeal stands before us. What the outcome will be, only time will tell. Have we kept enough of our own lore and wisdom to be able to overcome the centuries of destruction and self-misunderstanding? Will we be able to make use of what we have kept? Will our gods return to rule the day that is now dawning? The answers to these questions are set, and are being set; they were set in years past, and they are being set and re-set as you read these words.

The *Edda* tells us that the gods return, and that whatever the nature of their downfall, they always return in some form. But they might fight for their return, and we must fight alongside them. In every fight there is the risk of defeat, yet we see that the gods are still with us; and we have done much more than merely remember them. We see that the gods and goddesses are living beings and, on some level, as growing, changing beings they were/are always being destroyed and reborn. So we await a new level of their being. But this will not happen without our help, because in a real sense we and the gods are one; our doings are the surest signs of the workings of the gods themselves.

So what say the runestaves of Hœnir as the way of the gods is re-cast across the great unknown sea of being? These staves tell of great dreams. In these dreams the sons and daughters of Midgard first rekindle the flame of the gods within their hearts, and the flame within each individual is then brought together with those of kindred souls, which are gathered 'round hearths and within garths and hofs. The flame from each true man and woman feeds the flame of all the fellows—and into this warm hall the gods return out of the cold. The Troth will be satisfied with nothing less than the *re-establishment* of the Troth as the natural religion within this culture. We will not be satisfied with being a merely tolerated group of eccentrics getting together in suburban living rooms, congratulating ourselves on being born to this folk and badmouthing everyone else.

In the Troth to come, the runestaves are read to mean that we can have a hof in every major city in the English-speaking world, each hof having its own hof-elder or elders whose work it is to teach the folk and to give the blessings through which the gods and goddesses are further strengthened. On the blood-lots the runes are read to mean that great garths will be set up in the countryside, wherein good and true men and women will gather themselves to live and work for the betterment of the folk and the whole world. Come what may, it is from these garths that our good will and true will be sent forth, and it is within these garths that our work will bear its most shining fruit. Upon the stave the runes can be read to mean that there will arise a great and learned troop of wise and true folk, who will go forth into the world to rebuild that which has been lost. These will be known as the elders of the Troth; they will work as theals in the great blessings, and they will be the teachers of the lore among the folk. The runes are read to mean that throughout the depth and breadth of the land families will return to the Troth of their forebears. Many will see the truth within themselves and will return to it in their own homes, and with time these flames around the hearth will gather with the kindred and a new world will be brought forth.

These "dreams," these runic visions, have a practical set of guidelines by which they will be made into reality. Some of them are printed in the third part of this book, but most make up the program of the Elders of the Troth and its Ring of High Rede. What is most important right now is to realize that you may hold the most important tools for making these visions become reality: a key to the lore of the folk, and a heart with the will to work the blessings of the gods and goddesses. If you do not yet think of yourself as true, it is now time that you think deeply on what is in this book; if you already think of yourself as true, keep working with a renewed heart and mind. The Troth stands ready to help you and your family in your quest.

Part II
Working True

24

True Work

As has already been said in several ways, the Troth is a way of *doing*. It is in the actual workings that one does, in both everyday and holy settings, that a man or woman is really determined to be true. To *be* true one must *work* true.

In this second part of the book we will outline the things one needs to know in order to begin this true working. The watchword here will be simplicity. We will only be going into the basic things one needs to know to begin on the road to the Troth. Too many people get caught up in the technical details, which hinders their beginning and eventual progress. We will talk about the tools one needs to begin and the timing to be thought about when undertaking the blessings. Most importantly, we will outline the basic procedures and formulas used in building traditional workings, so that you can begin at work to improvise while familiar with a traditional framework.

Here we will also present a complete set of rituals which the one true man or woman can use to begin working true. The texts for kindred workings are also included, so that persons already working in groups can effectively begin to quicken and revive the spirit of the Troth in a highly traditional manner.

The formulaic outlines in chapter 26 are the real mainstays of the tradition. These basic formulas are *known* to have been the traditional ones used in the "Viking Age." Of course, the most important texts included here are those for the eight blessings of the year. Remember, to call one's self true, one must minimally take part in the blessings of the Winter Nights, Yule and Easter.

Above all it is the holy work of each true man and woman to be true in all that they do. Although the first emphasis is laid on what is done in the outer world, this is really only a framework upon which inner events and inner truths are hung. The true work is done in the heart of each true man and woman, but without the outer work there is no sign of it, and no bringing of its results and fruits into the realm of Midgard. It is, after all, the unique work of mankind to bring the truth into the realm of Midgard and to spread it here. The work within and the work without go hand in hand.

In much that will be read in this part of the book, the emphasis will be on *tradition*. However, I would like to point out that part of the tradition of the Troth lies in individual innovation. Do not be shy about varying elements of these rituals, or of eventually creating your own rites. What are presented here are only examples of what can be done. All are encouraged to practice for some time with standard workings, and only after that to begin to "innovate." Even after such innovation has begun, deviation from the formulaic elements presented in chapter 26 is discouraged, as far as the great blessings are concerned.

Another vital part of working true is spreading the word about the existence and nature of the Troth and the Ring of Troth. In this every true man and woman can help in the great work of the Hammer of Thunar as it swings out in ever wider rings to spread the truth of the gods and goddesses of the North. We in the Ring of Troth do not recommend proselytizing in any form. It is not our job or intention to "convert" anyone to our way. It is, however, our work to make information about the existence of the Troth available to all who might be interested in it.

The Troth is a *folk religion*. As such it is the birthright of all who belong to the folk. It follows then that it is not some kind of "secret order" to be kept hidden and obscure within closed "cell structures." There is an open door into the garden of the Troth, and all who feel that they belong to our folk shall be welcome to enter freely and of their own will.

25

Tools and Setting

In the performance of the rites and rituals of the Troth, the true individual will have to have a minimum set of tools with which to work. Ideally these should be items that are only used for holy purposes, but domestic items may be substituted in the beginning. Remember, the important thing is to begin working and to keep working. The fact that a blessing is performed is the important thing; that it was performed with the holiest of tools and weapons only increases its *quality*. If faced with the "choice" between working with special tools and not working at all, the answer is, as always, *work*!

Special tools become more necessary when working in groups (kindreds or hearths of the Ring of Troth). This is because the symbolic and transpersonal quality of the tools themselves will help to make the blessing more meaningful for all. This is also why "domestic" tools are acceptable for individual or domestic workings.

In this chapter, we will consider the actual tools used in workings of the Troth, as well as the overall setting of such workings, and the times when workings are best undertaken. For this final point, the reader is also referred to chapter 9: *The Year* for a complete discussion of the holy calendar.

Tools of the Troth

Most workings will make use of the tools discussed below. Certain special rites may involve others, but they will be discussed in those places. Here are the basic tools a true man or woman needs to begin working within a kindred or hearth today.

A hammer-token should be worn when doing any true work. For those who choose to work within the Ring of Troth, a special hammer-token will be available; for those who prefer to work on their own, of course, any sort of hammer-token will do.

A harrow (altar) should be set up upon which all holy work is undertaken. This harrow may, of course, be indoors or outside. Indoor harrows are usually made of wood (tables are most often used), and should be at least two feet by two feet; but any dimension will do. It is preferable if this object is used for holy work only. If the harrow is outside, it is usually made of stone. However, the indoor harrow can also be moved outdoors for rites that are best performed in that environment. Indoor harrows are also called stalls.

On the harrow there will usually be four items: the horn (or cup), the blessing bowl, the evergreen tine (twig), and the vessel of liquid (usually mead, ale, or beer), arranged as shown in figure 25.1.

The horn is a very traditional vessel from which to drink the holy draught during the working of the blessing. However, a cup or chalice may also be used for this purpose.

The blessing bowl should be made of wood, and should be large enough so that it will hold approximately half of the contents of the horn or cup being used. For indoor rites there is also to be an auxiliary bowl, which is placed on the floor to the side of the harrow. This auxiliary bowl will

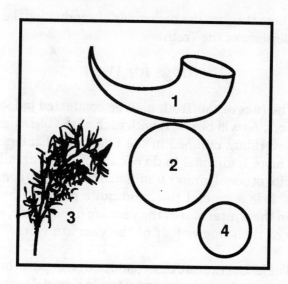

Figure 25.1: The Harrow Arrangement

receive the outpouring of the liquid, which in outdoor rites would be poured out onto the ground. The contents of this other bowl are then solemnly poured out onto the ground outside after the conclusion of the working.

The tine or evergreen twig is to be freshly cut for every blessing from some conifer tree or bush. It is normally placed on the ground (or in the auxiliary bowl) and marks the spot where the final outpouring of the sanctified liquid is to take place. It is, of course, primarily used as a tool with which to sprinkle the harrow and kindred with the holy liquid—to actually do the blessing.

The vessel containing the liquid to be used in the blessing should be a special one. It will be used to pour the mead, ale, or beer into the horn, before it is circulated and hallowed. This vessel is usually an earthenware bottle or jar.

These then are the basic tools of conducting the rites and blessings of the Troth.

Settings for Work

The rites of the Troth may be conducted indoors or outdoors. As will be noted with each of the blessings and other workings outlined in the following chapters, it is often more traditional to do certain of the rites indoors, while for others it is more traditional to conduct them outdoors. It is a general rule, and quite natural, that the rites in the winter half of the year are done inside, while those of the summer half of the year are worked outside.

The indoor rites are best conducted on a special harrow used only for that purpose and set up in a special part of the house or apartment. It is best if you can have the harrow set up in a permanent way as a shrine to the gods and goddesses of the folk. But it is quite acceptable to store the holy tools of the Troth in a way showing them respect, and to bring them out only at times when holy work is to be undertaken.

The outdoor rites can, of course, be held in one's own yard, which is perhaps the best of all places for such workings from the standpoint of sacred significance. But other outdoor settings are also quite fine. Many true rites are held in parks, woods, and fields in the countryside. The advantage to setting up a harrow on one's own property is obvious. The stones upon which the blessings are given take on an increasingly holy aspect every time blessings are held on them. In time they become holy themselves. But when working in open land, any natural object, or even a portable wooden harrow, can be used for conducting the rites.

Timing

In chapter 9 the traditional timing of the greater and lesser blessings of the year were given. There it was also noted that these dates were in many cases approximate and often governed by local conditions and traditions. In the Troth today there is just as much reason for having flexible and locally determined times for the working of the rites as there was in nights of yore. They are perhaps different reasons often determined by socio-economic factors rather than by factors having to do with the cycles of nature. But the socio-economic forces are no less real in our lives today than the natural circumstances were to our ancestors. In fact, they work in the same way in our lives. They are the cycles of production of the means by which we live. These should be taken into consideration when setting the time for a blessing or other event of the Troth.

In determining a tide for the holding of a holy event such factors as time needed and time available should be considered. If the blessing and sumble and all the other events planned are going to take several hours to prepare and conduct, it would be unwise to hold it on a weeknight when most of the fellows in the kindred will have to work the next day. This factor is, of course, less important when working alone.

In absolute terms there are three ways to determine the best time for holding a blessing or other get-together: 1) traditional/mechanical time (that is, determined by events in the heavens—the solstice, equinox, and so forth); 2) traditional/organic (that is, a local custom of having, for example, the Easter blessing on the first Friday or Saturday night/morning after the appearance of a robin redbreast, or violet); and 3) taking into account the general timing determined by the heavenly events in order to set a time convenient for most of the folks involved.

26

Ways of Working

Common Procedures in the
Rite of the Troth

In the texts of the rites presented in the following chapters there are, as in all rites involving deep traditions, many elements that will be repeated. These are the elements that give a timeless and traditional orientation to much of what is done. We will speak about these elements here in some detail, so that we will not have to repeat them over and over, and so that they can be presented in a clear and understandable manner. It is the right and true understanding and doing of some of these traditional elements that great power can be poured into the work.

Besides this, we will present the basic structural formulas of the blessing and the sumble, from which the individual true folk can construct their own rites in an authentically traditional manner. This kind of formulaic outline is the true essence of the Germanic tradition—basic continuity with the ever-present possibility of creative innovation. Again, all true men and women are encouraged to experiment and to share their experiments in true work with others in the Troth; but all should remain with the basic formulas shown here to ensure the revitalization and continuance of our traditions.

The basic formula of the blessing follows a ninefold plan:

Name	Function
1) Hallowing	sets ritual space/time apart from ordinary
2) Reading	puts rite into mythic context
3) Rede	links myth to purpose of rite
4) Call	invokes deities or classes of beings
5) Loading	charges drink with godly power
6) Drinking	circulates godly power within
7) Blessing	circulates godly power without
8) Giving	returns rightful part of power to divinity
9) Leaving	declares work rightly done/return to ordinary

All workings outlined in this book can be performed with a single celebrant, who is always designated with the term "speaker" in the texts. However, in kindred settings it is usually best if several persons take an active part in the working of the rite. The roles can be divided as the kindred leader sees fit. The most traditional type of division of work would be into three roles, called 1) theal, 2) shope, and 3) goodman. The theal is responsible for all speaking parts that involve calling on the divine powers and distributing their blessings. The shope is responsible for all speaking parts involving the setting of mythic and social context. The goodman is responsible for all of the non-speaking ritual actions having to do with the actual distribution of the holy liquid. A modification of this use, especially when the "theal" role is assumed by a Troth Elder, or by one in training, is for the goodman to take the speaking roles, allowing the theal to undertake the ritual actions of distributing the holy liquid. These are, however, only suggestions. Any permutation of these roles can be practiced.

In the beginning of most workings the speaker is instructed to strike the holy posture indicated by the rune [Y]. To do this one simply stands straight with the arms straight out and up at approximately a 45° angle, simulating the runestave shape. This is an ancient pose used by the Teutonic peoples when coming into communication with their gods and goddesses; it was even noted by the Romans. When the sign [Y] occurs in the ritual texts, the speaker should strike this pose.

The Hammer-Working

The normal way to hallow a stead, or sanctify a place, for holy work is by means of the hammer-working. This sets the place apart from the outside, everyday, profane world, making it special and outside ordinary time/space. In this especially prepared space/time, holy work can be rightly done. To perform the hammer-working, one faces north and makes the sign of the hammer [⊥] by tracing it in the air, imagining it to be drawn in space, hovering in the air to the north of the holy site. (See figure 26.1) While doing this the speaker says: "Hammer in the north! Hold and hallow this stead!" This process is repeated in the east, south, and west. Then the speaker returns to the north and looks upward, tracing the hammer sign high above the ritual site, and says: "Hammer above me [or us]! Hold and hallow this stead!" Then the speaker looks below and again makes the sign, visualizing it deep below the ritual site, and says: "Hammer below me [or us]! Hold and hallow this stead!" Thus the site is surrounded by six hammer signs. These will guard the stead from disturbing forces, but will make it attractive and hospitable to the gods, goddesses, and all other friendly wights.

Common Procedures

In the fifth part of the blessing formula, when the holy drink is loaded with the invoked force, the speaker first takes up the horn or cup in his or her left hand and then with the right hand pours the liquid from the vessel into the horn or cup.

When anyone drinks from a horn or cup, they usually make the sign of the hammer or some other holy sign over the rim of the drinking vessel. This is done with either the whole hand or the index and/or middle finger. When doing this, the person should actually see the sign of the hammer, or another sign, appear over the drink and shine its light into the liquid. The hammer-sign is made in the way shown in figure 26.1.

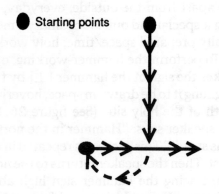

Figure 26.1: The Hammer-sign

The hammer-sign is also used for general blessings of food, drink, and individuals.

During the sixth part of the blessing, when the gathered folk are drinking of the loaded mead or ale, it is most usual for each individual to take a moderate mouthful of the liquid and to swallow it slowly in three swallows, each time feeling the power of the loaded liquid coursing through the entire body. If a large number of folk are gathered, it may be necessary to empty the horn or cup into the blessing bowl before all have drunk. (The horn should be emptied into the blessing bowl on the harrow once its contents are about one-half to two-thirds gone.) In such instances, the speaker merely refills the horn from the vessel, makes the hammer-sign over its rim, and continues the distribution of the liquid, again pouring out the contents when it becomes low, into the blessing bowl. An alternate way of distributing the liquid is to have each participant drink half of the contents of the horn, and have the speaker empty the other half into the blessing bowl. This process is repeated for each person present. When all have drunk of the liquid, the contents of the horn or cup are poured into the blessing bowl slowly and with great care.

Part seven of the blessing, the actual sprinkling (or blessing itself), is usually carried out by the speaker by dipping the evergreen tine into the liquid in the blessing bowl, and slowly going around the harrow three times, sprinkling the harrow on all four sides while repeating the words appropriate to that blessing. At the conclusion of each turn around the harrow the tine is again dipped into the liquid. The harrow is a symbol for all of Midgard, and as such is the first phase of the blessing. Here the powers of the gods and goddesses are given into the world. If the speaker is working with an indoor stall, and it is not possible to go around it on all sides, the stall is simply sprinkled on three sides as the speaker stands before it. However, it is still customary for the tine to be dipped three times.

In the eighth part of the blessing, the liquid is poured from the blessing bowl standing on the harrow out onto the ground, if the rite is being done outdoors, or into the auxiliary bowl to the right or left of the stall, if the rite is conducted indoors. After the rite is concluded, the contents of the auxiliary bowl are taken outdoors and poured out onto the bare ground in a solemn manner.

The Sumble

The sumble, or ritual feast, usually follows the Great Blessings of the Year. The sumble is a special holy working in its own right, and deserves a good deal of attention from those who wish to work truly. (The word *sumble* is derived from the Icelandic *sumbl* and the Old English *symbel*, meaning religious drinking ritual or ritual feast.) It is a coming together of the folk for partaking in the godly ale. It is most often the case that after the blessing the participants retire to another location (ideally a banquet hall) for the performance of the sumble. Sumbles can also be performed alone, independent of a blessing.

The sumble is an imitation of the ritual feasts held by the gods and goddesses in Asgard. Once the sumble has begun, the participants enter into a realm of divine time/space. They enter into the stream of timeless continuity, where the events of the past can be ritually bound to the events to come, thus reshaping the "future" in the image of the idealized "past." There is obviously a powerful magic at work here. This is one of the ways in which the Teutonic metaphysic of time/space and of wyrd (see chapter 19) can be used in a practical way.

As the great blessings are a way to "bring the divine into the world," the sumble is a way to "maintain the stream of continuity from gods to men and through the generations of time." The sumble keeps the gods and heroes, including our own ancestors, alive and living among us. It is also that time for ritual boasts or oaths. These boasts are not only "bragging" about past accomplishments but also oaths concerning what one is to do in the time to come. They are a way of ritually and objectively putting before one's kith and kin (those whose respect you wish to have) what one intends to do. In the whole context of the sumble, one swears before the gods and goddesses, before one's kith and kin. Oaths sworn in this setting have great power, a power derived from many levels and sources.

In the sumble can be seen the origins of many of our profane drinking customs, such as "toasts." We can also see why we talk about drinking alcohol in "rounds."

The formula for the sumble follows a sixfold plan, but it is more open to innovation than is the formula for the blessings.

Name	Function
1) Seating	puts folk in right/holy order
2) Bringing of Horn	brings holy liquid into the hall
3) Beginning	invokes the purpose of the sumble
4) First Boasts	honors the gods and heroes
5) Other Boasts	works for individuals or groups
6) Leaving	closes rounds

As the sumble is not discussed elsewhere in this book, we must now describe it in some detail.

In a sumble, the gathered folk seat themselves in some significant manner or order. In nights of yore the head of the clan or chieftain would sit at the head of the table or in a high-seat, with those of highest authority under him closest to him. Those of less authority, or the younger members of the hall, would be seated further away from the head. Each kindred will probably have its own system, but it is ritually important to have some tradition in this regard as it increases the level of significance in the arrangement or context in which the actions will take place. After all have taken their

seats, a designated person, the leading woman of the kindred, or some special assistant to the kindred leader will
ceremonially bring in the first horn or cup of holy liquid
(mead, ale, or beer may be used) and set it down before the
leader. The leader/speaker then stands up and speaks a
formal opening to the sumble, such as: "We are rightly
gathered. Now we wend our way into the timeless realm
unseen, and share together in elder pathways to might
and main."

After this there is a series of formalized "boasts" (actually
drinks to the honor of the gods and ancestors). Of these we
have some remnants direct from Old Norse sources, but
they are piecemeal and unsystematic. Such boasts should
be drunk at least to Woden, Tiw, Thunar, Frey, and Freya,
followed by a general round honoring the forebears. Such a
series of formalized boasts could be:

1) "To Woden for good speed and wisdom!"
2) "To Tiw for wit and good Troth!"
3) "To Thunar for ward and thew!" (= strength)
4) "To Frey for feast and frith!"
5) "To Freya for freedom and frolic!"
6) "To our kinsmen whom we ken not, and to
   those beloved who are buried and burned
   [here repeat the names of dead relatives,
   etc.]!"

After the formalized boasts have been completed,
there begins an unlimited series of individualized boasts.
Each individual may use his or her own horn in drinking
the rounds, or a large ceremonial horn may actually be
passed around the table for all to drink from. The nature of
these individualized boasts varies from person to person.
Some will recount great mythic events, or offer historical
events with heroic dimensions of work in skaldic form;

while still others will make personal boasts (oaths) concerning things which they intend to bring about in the days to come.

When all have finished the rounds they have planned, and all wode (inspiration) is spent, the rounds are called to a halt by the leader/speaker with a formal declaration, such as: "I call the rounds ended. Let us wend our way back to our stead, back to our time, and go forth from here with mighty moods."

Blessings of the Gods and Goddesses

Here you have the two major formulas, that of the blessing and that of the sumble, which are needed to develop further rituals tailored to the needs of individuals and individual kindreds.

In this book you will not find a whole liturgy specific to a particular god or goddess. Cults dedicated to individual divinities are certainly practiced; however, it is not the place of the general Troth to dictate what forms these should take. It is also part of the "Mandate of Woden" that the great blessings be promoted over the individualized cults (which if overemphasized could lead to disintegration in the folk).

In order to make the formula of the blessing absolutely clear, we will include a "Blessing of Thunar" here just to show how the formula can be implemented. If the individual true man or woman feels a special link to a certain god or goddess (which is quite normal), that individual is really the best person to formulate a special blessing form dedicated to that deity.

A Blessing of Thunar

1. Hallowing
Perform the hammer-working, perhaps substituting the words "Hammer of Thunar, hold and hallow this stead!" for the usual words. Then say:

"I hallow this harrow to the honor of Thunar. Through the might and main of Mjollnir this stead is warded, as Thunar

wards the halls of Asgard against the wrath of Etins. Mjollnir hold out all unholy wights and sendings!"

2. Reading
Read or recite the "Lay of Hymir" from the *Poetic Edda*.

3. Rede

"*Let us think for a while upon the meaning of the lay which we have just heard, and upon the growing might of Thunar in our midst!*"

(After a few moments, the speaker may venture an interpretation of the deeper importance of the "Lay of Hymir.")

4. Call

"*Mighty Asa-Thunar, we hear thee roar in the hall of stars, we feel thy force in the thunder, we witness thy life in the lightning, we smell thy being in the time before the rain. In the storm we know that thou ridest eastward to do battle with the Etin Hoard. We wish thee good speed in the fray! Hear us as we again call forth in thy names:*

> *Eldest son of Woden!*   [After each name the
> *Thunderer!*   gathered folk can say "WE
> *Son of Erda!*   GIVE THEE WELCOME!"]
> *Redbeard!*
> *Father of Magni and Modhi!*
> *God of Goats!*

We call upon thee as in days of yore, and as the gods themselves when in need of thy ever-ready might!"

5. Loading
(The speaker pours ale into the horn, holds it aloft with the words:)

"We give thee great gifts! Not of blood, but of our mighty deeds, our strivings, our Troth housed in this ale. May it help us, gods and folk together, in our fight against those who would war against Asgard, or who would seek to bring grey slavery to Midgard. Thunar take well with our gifts, but not as from thralls, for we have no master, but as from thanes and as a sign of our kinship and fellowship."

6. Drinking

(The speaker makes the sign of the hammer over the rim of the horn and drinks from it. The horn is passed around to each sworn member of the kindred.)

7. Blessing

(Ale is finally poured into the blessing bowl on the harrow. The harrow and the sworn members of the kindred are blessed with the words:)

"The blessings of Thunar be upon you!"

8. Giving

(Ale is poured out on the ground to the east of the harrow with the words:)

"To Thunar, Warder of the world and trustworthy one in Asgard, and to Earth, Mother of Thunar, and of us all!"

9. Leaving

(Speaker returns to the harrow and faces north in the [ᛉ] posture and says:)

"Let us think deeply about what has happened here and what it means in our lives—

Now the work is wrought, and the gifts have been given, each to the other, as it must always be. May it strengthen our kindred, and renew in our hearts our will to live as worthy sons (and daughters) of Thunar. We swear to always hold good our oaths to our gods and kindred. So shall it be!"

27

Nightly Workings

Although not really essential to the true practice of the Troth, some folks like to orient themselves more regularly to the holy gods and goddesses than is done at the occasional times of blessings. For these good folk and true, there are the workings that are to be performed every day (and night) during the course of the day: upon rising, when donning the Hammer of Thunar, at noon, and upon going to sleep.

Greeting of Sunna

Each morning, upon rising, true folk can perform the "Greeting of Sunna," to greet the morning Sun and put themselves into the holy stream of power flowing from the goddess Sunna (the Sun). Rise, face east in the [**Ψ**] position and say:

"Hail Sunna, light of Har newly risen!
Hail to thee who shed light and life on all our forebears,
Who shines on us now, and who shall shine on all our
offspring yet unborn!
Share with me some of thy light and might this day, that
I may better fight in the fray and gain many goals!"

Hammer Signing

Another holy work that can be done at any time, but which should follow right after the "Greeting of Sunna," is the hammer signing. In this work, true folk can reach up into the holy light and might of the gods and make it a part of themselves. To begin, the person should visualize a bright shining ball of golden light two or three feet above the head. Then with the right hand reach up into that light and make a fist, grasping the light-substance in the hand, which should then be drawn down to the forehead. Touch your forehead and say: "Tiw!" Then continue to pull the light down through the head and touch the mouth and say: "Woden!" Next, draw the light down in a column through the body and touch the solar plexus, and say: "Thunar!" Then, move the fist, and the light contained in it, from the solar plexus to the left shoulder; touch the shoulder and say: "Frey!" Now, drawing the light across the body in a horizontal direction, touch the light to the right shoulder and say: "Freya!"

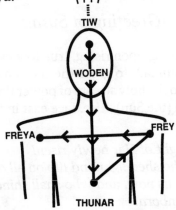

Figure 27.1: The Hammer-Sign in the Body

Other Workings

A further daily working relating to the hammer is the hammer-donning ceremony. This is really just a simple affirmation of will and troth that is repeated when the true man or woman puts their hammer-token on each day. It is, of course, quite common for true folk to habitually wear the hammer-token, either in a way that all can see or under their clothing. In either case, when it is put on, it is good to repeat a simple word-spell, such as: "This day shall bring new wonders, great doings, boundless luck and happiness unending—by the might of the hammer!" It is perhaps most effective if this is said while holding the hammer-token out in front of you at about eye-level; when you place the hammer around your neck, you can then feel the power that is loaded into it spread throughout your being.

The food that one eats at any time during the day can always be blessed with the sign of the hammer. In each case the might and main of the hammer—its vitality and strength—are projected into the actual food.

At the noon-tide, true folk may greet and honor the Sun, as she has reached her highest point in the heavens. Her victory is saluted with the simple word-spell: "Hail Sunna, in the highest dwelling of heaven!" When doing this it is best to be outdoors, standing in the [ᛉ] posture.

Finally, when the true man or woman is going to sleep, he or she should perhaps repeat a word-spell of special personal importance in an attempt to call upon the realm of sleep to bestow dreams of might and main.

28

Workings of the Life-Tides

"Rites of Passage"

Throughout the life of any man or woman there are tides, moments in time, when great transformations take place. These take place when one comes into the world and is made part of the community of the clan in Midgard; when one reaches the age of maturity as a true man or woman and can be held fully responsible for one's deeds and doings; when one gets married; and finally upon death when one makes the final journey of life across the span between Midgard to the realms beyond. These tides are seen as significant points in life and as changes that are best undergone with the help of holy workings.

Beyond these major transformations, there may also be two other moments of similar importance. One comes when a family (or individual) moves from one house to another. When this happens, a rite of "land-taking" should be performed to make the land one's own. Also, if a true man or woman wants to confirm themselves in the Troth, and he or she is not able to be a part of a kindred, hearth, garth, or hof, he or she can perform a lone working of becoming true.

Naming

When a child is born to a true man and woman, the couple should wait nine days before ceremonially naming the child. This will give wyrd a chance to determine whether the child is indeed a healthy part of the organic stream of humanity. On the evening of the ninth night, the mother will give the child over to the father for blessing and naming. The father seats himself on a chair before the family stall or harrow, and the mother brings the child and hands it to the seated father. He takes it and lays it on his lap, cradling its head in the crook of his left arm. He takes pure spring water, sprinkles it on the head of the child, and gives it its name by saying: *"I sprinkle this child with water and give him/her the name* _____ , *after his/her* _____ [here mention the relation to the child of the person after whom it is named])." An example of this would be, *"I sprinkle this child with water and give her the name Helga after her grandmother."* In this way the trust we have in rebirth is practically confirmed, and in this way the father gives birth to the soul of the child, just as surely as the mother gave birth to its lyke. Some symbolic gift is usually bestowed on the child as a way to bind the name to it. A small Thorr's hammer is ideal.

In naming children, true parents should keep several things in mind. They should try to give names of Teutonic derivation (or give middle names of this sort). Also, of course, names of dead ancestors should be continued. Here all of the names of the ancestors can be considered. If they had a middle name of Teutonic origin (which may have been their *real* name, in the sense that it carried their soul), that one should be used in the child's name also.

Becoming a Man or Woman

This rite can be as complex or as simple as local custom and family tradition dictate. Within the lore of the Troth, however, it is a time that should be marked by some working. The timing of this may vary, but it will come between the ages of twelve and eighteen. In the most elaborate forms of such rites, there are protracted and dramatic ordeals to be undergone in secrecy. These are again determined within a local context, and anyway could not be printed in a book for public consumption due to their secret and mysterious natures. However, what is important in such rites is that the father of a son or the mother of a daughter give a gift symbolic of the transition of the offspring to the state of manhood or womanhood. In the case of a boy, this is usually a symbolic weapon of some sort. A sword would perhaps be the most powerful symbol. These swords or other objects can also be handed down as heirlooms, and are most powerful when they mark the continuity of the name-soul. It is then seen how the fetch actually "rides" into the lives of the offspring through these symbolic objects. In the case of a girl, the object is usually a belt ("girdle") or necklace, from which are hung tokens (usually of precious metals and stones) of the past generations. These are, of course, also handed down from generation to generation and confirm the continuity of the clan.

Wedding

Elders of the Ring of Troth are legally empowered by the laws of the land to conduct the rites of marriage. There are various ritual formulas by which this can be done. However, in the absence of such an official ceremony, the true man and woman may also conduct a private rite between themselves which is both simple and powerful.

In the private rite, a ring is drawn on the ground around a harrow or before an indoor stall. On the harrow are two cups or horns and two finger rings. The man enters the ring from the west, the wife from the east, and they both step before the harrow, facing one another. She gives him a horn on the right, swearing her love for the man and asking him if he will take well with this love. He responds that he will. Then he repeats this offering of the horn while swearing of love and requesting acceptance. Then the rings are exchanged. Here the man puts the ring on the wife's finger, swearing his loyalty to her—"*I plight my troth in thee.*" The wife then repeats the actions towards the man with similar oaths. Once these exchanges are complete, the man and wife embrace and kiss.

When a Troth Elder presides over a wedding, the ceremony is of a different nature. The couple stand before the Elder with their witnesses standing to their sides. The Elder asks who will speak for the bride, whereupon her witness speaks good words in her behalf (concerning her qualities); then the Elder asks the witness of the groom to do the same. Both are then asked to swear their will to marry and to plight their troth in one another. The couple are then blessed with the sign of the hammer, after which general blessings of all the gods and goddesses are called down onto the couple by the Elder. After the rite is concluded there follows a great celebratory feast.

In the traditional literature we see a reflection of the official ceremony in the "Lay of Thrym" in the *Poetic Edda*; the rite conducted in private between a man and woman is reflected in the *Völsunga Saga* and in the "Lay of Sigrdrifa" (as well as in the *Poetic Edda*).

Land-Taking

In our highly mobile society we find ourselves moving and taking up new abodes quite often. This is in many ways similar to the wanderings of the folk during the semi-nomadic periods in its history. We often feel the negative effects of this lifestyle in the form of alienation. Our ancestors had a ritual way of alleviating this. It was the rite of "land-taking" (Old Norse: *landnáma*). This rite can be used for houses on lots, as well as for apartments. However, it should be done without fail and for pieces of property which true folk have actually bought and own.

In the first part of the work, the land is marked off and warded by taking fire around the edges of the land or building. Then the wights of the stead are called on to be friendly and to help in keeping the house in frith and well-being.

The speaker, holding a torch, fire-pot, or lantern, stands before the front door of the house or at the edge of the property and says:

"I am come to take up this land and all dwellings on it in the name(s) of (here the names of those owning or living on the property are to be cited) *and in the names of the gods and goddesses of our folk."*

Then the speaker makes the sign of the hammer [⊥], and says:

"The hammer of Thunar hallow this land and ward it well."

The speaker then begins to walk around the property in a clockwise direction while carrying the fire. If more than one person is actually taking the land, a relay can be set up in which the fire is handed to the other person(s) stationed at intervals around the land. While walking the edge of the land, the words *"By troth the land is taken and well it is warded"* are spoken.

The speaker, again standing in the stead where he or she began, sets the fire down before the front door or at the gate of the property and says:

"Glad greetings and hail to all you wights that dwell in this stead! We give you honor as in the days and nights of yore. Let there be among us frith and grith and, and naught of strife!"

Here the speaker drinks a sip from a horn of ale and pours the rest onto the ground before the dwelling (or into an auxiliary bowl in the case of an apartment), and says: *"Come ye wights to get the gifts due to you! Bring ye wealth and weal, merry wit and mirth to this home!"*

The work is ended with the words: *"Now the work is wrought, may this home and all that dwell herein know naught but good as long as the Troth has abode within!"*

Those taking possession of the land should now enter it and live in frith and grith with the helpful wights of the dwelling.

Death

Rites for the dead can be officially conducted by an Elder of the Ring of Troth, or they can be simply conducted by the family of the dead man or woman. There are two major variations for the way in which the lyke is treated after death: burial and burning. It is more usual for those who were dedicated to the Wanes to be buried and those dedicated to one or more of the Ases to be cremated. In either case the usual final resting place of the remains are in a burial site, accompanied by grave goods. Grave goods can be actual objects that the person cherished in life, or symbols of these. Traditional symbolic items would include food and drink (preferably grains, and mead, ale, or beer).

Other items would be particular to the needs of the person in the remanifestations of the fetch and/or myne-hugh to come—weapons, magical tools, jewels, gold, and so forth. Each of these items, just like the body being interred, has a subtle essence as well as an outer physical form. It is in the subtle, symbolic qualities that the true importance of the grave goods are to be found.

Troth Elders are empowered to conduct the rites for the dead in consultation with the family and clan of the dead man or woman. For some, a grave or memorial stone bearing runes and carved by a true runemaster may be felt to be appropriate. (For details on both of these services, the reader should write to the Ring of Troth.)

The ritual formula for the funeral rites consists of five parts: 1) a hallowing (in which the grave site is made holy); 2) a call to the gods and goddesses to whom the dead person was dedicated; 3) the sending of the dead on his or her way and the bidding of a fond farewell; 4) the drinking of the first myne-cup (a toast drunk to their memory, such as would be drunk in a sumble); and 5) the leaving, in which all bid a farewell to the departed. In the drinking of the myne-cup of horn, the worthy deeds and other words of honor are spoken by one or more speakers. This is most often to be done by a man's eldest son, or a woman's eldest daughter.

The raising of a runestone in memory of the person is also accompanied by many rites and ceremonies. These usually are conducted nine months to a year after the date of the person's death.

29

Kindred Workings

A true kindred can be started by any group of people who want to work true to the gods and goddesses of the North. The rites and workings contained in this book are more than enough to start and maintain a kindred. (A kindred is distinguished from a hearth within the Ring of Troth only in that the hearth has official sanction of the Ring, and is part of its network of hearths, garths and hofs.) Of course, we would welcome those who read this book to become affiliated with the Ring of Troth and encourage groups to apply for official status within the Ring, but such things are not absolutely necessary.

In this chapter you will find out how to ceremonially found a kindred, how to open and close kindred meetings in an effective manner, and how to conduct a rite for inducting a new member into the kindred. Every kindred—every hearth and garth—will develop rites and rituals particular to itself. This is to be expected and encouraged. What appears here is a minimal set of workings to get a kindred started.

Every kindred ought to have a special holy object; a ring is most usual if the kindred is headed by a godhi or gydhja, but it could also be a stone or other symbolic object, which embodies the whole of the kindred and its members in all their depth and being. This object should be situated on the harrow or stall each time the kindred meets or holds a working. It is upon this object that members of the kindred will most effectively swear their oaths. It is also most effective if the kindred has a name of some kind. This can be an imaginative name, or one merely describing the geographical location.

Founding a Kindred

To found a kindred, a general blessing to honor all the gods and goddesses of the Troth together should be held. During the Rede part of the working, the speaker should announce that as a part of the purpose of the rite, a kindred is to come into being; (and the speaker may add whatever else he or she thinks it right to say about the kindred and its members). At the time of the Blessing, the speaker adds the words: "*And upon this harrow* (or *stall) and upon this* (name the most holy token) *is quickened and made fast the* (here name the kindred)."

Opening a Kindred Meeting

The kindred will, of course, get together on many occasions at which no formal blessing, sumble, or any other kind of working will be done. However, to keep the holy significance of the gatherings firmly in mind, a short blessing is to be done. All the gathered folk make the sign of the hammer, and a designated speaker faces north in the [**Y**] position, and says something such as:

"*All hail the high gods   From the north a harrying
We call upon you wondrous wights
Our deeds and doings   This night/day to hallow
Tiw our words to witness,*

> *Woden to give us wisdom,*
> *Thunar to ward us well,*
> *Freya and Frey our thoughts to free!"*

[At this point in some meetings a liquid libation may be distributed to the gathered folk, and boasts can be drunk to the gods and goddesses. In any case the opening concludes with the words:]

> *"May our words be wise and mighty our moods!"*

Before parting, the meeting is called to an end with another simple blessing such as:

> *"Rightly have we gathered in the gladness of the Troth. Now may all wend their ways homeward in wisdom and well-being!"*

Work of Coming into a Kindred

The work of coming into a kindred is the most special rite of a kindred, because it is very much like bringing a new member into the clan. It is the final retaking of the soul of the true man or woman back into the stream of life from which his ancestors were torn. The "oath of the gods" is a reversal of the oaths the European Saxons were forced to swear in forsaking their own gods. Here the true reclaim their birthrights!

The harrow is set up in the usual fashion, with a bowl of spring water and the most holy token of the kindred, and a chair or stool situated to the south of the harrow or stall.

1. The Hammer-Working is done.

2. Oath of the Gods and Goddesses.

The speaker (kindred leader) stands facing the prospective kindred member, who stands facing north on the south side of the harrow. (If done with a free-standing harrow, the speaker is to stand on the north side of the harrow with the prospective member on the south side of it, facing the speaker across the harrow on the north.)

Speaker:	*"Forsakest thou the angels of alienation?"*
Candidate:	*"I forsake the angels of alienation!"*
Speaker:	*"And all the services of the White-Christ?"*
Candidate:	*"I forsake all the services of the White-Christ!"*
Speaker:	*"And all the Christian works?"*
Candidate:	*"And I forsake all the works and words of the so-called father, and his son named Jesus, and their unholy spirit!"*

(This first part of the rite can be omitted if it is felt to be unnecessary.)

Speaker:	*"Trustest thou in the mighty All-father?"*
Candidate:	*"I trust in Woden, the mighty All-father!"*
Speaker:	*"Trustest thou in Thunar, warder of the world?"*
Candidate:	*"I trust in Thunar, warder of the world!"*
Speaker:	*"Trust thou in Freya and Frey, the lady and lord of our folk?"*
Candidate:	*"I trust in the Lord and Lady of our folk!"*

(In this second part of the oath, the gods and goddesses can be rewritten to reflect the particular allegiances of the candidate.)

3. Naming.

The speaker sits on the chair facing east, and the candidate sits on his or her lap or on another chair before this speaker facing the north. The speaker takes up the bowl of water and sprinkles some on the head of the candidate, with the words:

"I throw water upon this sib newly born, and give him/her the name (here the person's name[s] are recited) *after* [. . .]."

[If the sibling is being named after a certain ancestor or hero, this should be added to the formula.]

4. Oath of the Kindred.

[This oath should best be specially formulated for each individual kindred. It should be sworn on the most holy token of the kindred. If the kindred is headed by one who is considered a godhi or gydhja, it should be sworn on his or her ring. Here is an example of an oath taken from the Austin Kindred of the Ásatrú Free Assembly from around 1980:]

"Upon this ring of the kindred I swear by all the holy gods and goddesses to hold ever high the banner of the raven and always to help the growth and well-being of the kindred and of all the subs within it. By Woden and Tiw I swear this oath!"

5. Rede of the Speaker.

[This is a specially written charge to the new sibling, a personalized speech which expresses the hopes of the speaker for the sibling, and his or her destiny within the kindred.]

6. Self-Oath.

[This is to be composed by the new sibling and to be read aloud at this time, as an expression of his or her will within the kindred, of the way he or she has chosen, and of the things they will bring to the kindred.]

A blessing or sumble may now be held to honor the newly received sibling of the kindred.

30

The Great, Greater and Greatest Blessings of the Troth

The Turning of the Year

The Greatest Blessing of the Winter Nights (October 13-15).

The Blessing of the Dises

The harrow or stall is to be set up in the usual manner. This rite is usually performed by a female Elder, or *gydhja* ("priestess"), which is the most traditional method. Also, the use of ale (or beer) is more traditional to workings involving the feminine aspects.

1. Hallowing
The hammer-working is wrought to ward the stead and make it holy, after which the speaker says:

"Thus this stead is hallowed for our work here tonight. As the god Heimdall wards the Bifrost Bridge, so this stead is warded against all unholy wights and ways."

2. Reading
The Völuspá from the *Poetic Edda*.

3. Rede
The speaker, in the [ᛦ] posture, says:

> *"Hail ye Holy Ides   Dises of the Harrow,*
> *Hold ye whole the kindred:*
> *Mighty mothers of old   Turn our minds toward you!*
> *Wend ye nigh these winter nights!"*

4. Call
The speaker lowers his or her arms, turns to the gathered folk and says:

"Tonight we name the winter night and call forth the dises of the kindred. Ye have been known by many names, ye great mothers of our folk who ever drive us forward to more daring deeds, and to more fruitful fields—

O, ye spae-ides, ye wondrous womanly wights all-weird, we call you:

> *Jodis of the horse,*
> *Hjordis of the sword,*
> *Valdis of the slain*
> *Vigdis of battle,*
> *Asdis of the Ases,*
> *Irmundis of the fight,*
> *Herdis of the host!"*

5. Loading
Again turning to face the harrow (to the north), the speaker pours ale into the horn or other drinking vessel, and holds it aloft, saying:

"We give this ale, blended with awe, to you O mighty mothers all-old!"

6. Drinking

The horn is then individually handed to each true man and woman gathered before the harrow. The folk are to drink half of the contents of the horn, and the speaker is to return the undrunk part of the ale to the harrow, where it is poured into the blessing bowl. As each true man or woman is handed the horn, he or she makes the hammer-sign over its rim, and may speak a spell from the heart on the coming year.

7. Blessing

Once the process of handing the horn around is complete, the speaker stands before the harrow and makes the sign of ⊥ and 卐 over the center of the blessing bowl, while intoning the holy words:

"This ale is hallowed to the dises of the kindred and of the folk."

The speaker then circles the harrow three times with the Sun, all the while sprinkling the harrow itself with the ale from the evergreen bough. While doing this he or she should say:

"To all the dead dises and to all the awesome ides!"

Then, in a very pointed manner, the speaker should directly sprinkle first the members of the kindred, then all known good folk and true. If any gathered are known to be uncommitted to the Troth, sprinkling them should be avoided.

8. Giving

The speaker now removes the blessing bowl from the harrow, takes it to a point just north of the harrow, and pours its contents out upon the bare ground with the words:

"Holy mothers of men, Holy mothers of women,
Weird daughters of Woden
To you we give this ale!"

9. Leaving

Again the speaker returns to his or her original place before the harrow, faces northward with arms aloft and says:

"From these nights to the Twelfth Night of Yule, the walls between the worlds of the dises all-dead, and of us all-living here, grows ever thinner—may the wisdom of these weird women, all-loving, become known to all here tonight! Let us now go forth and make merry, for the year is young!"

The Blessing of the Elves

In addition to the Blessings of the Dises, a Blessing of the Elves can also be performed on the Winter Nights. The procedure is identical to that of the Blessing of the Dises; however, the speeches in points 3), 4), 5), 7), 8), and 9) should read:

3) *"Hail the holy Elves,   Shining of the harrow,*
Whole ye hold the kindred,
Mighty elders of old   Turn our minds toward you!"

4) *"Tonight we name the winter night and call forth the elder elves of the kindred. Ye have been known by many names, ye great elders of our folk who ever lead us to greater lore, and fare us to more fruitful fields.*
O, ye Light-elves above and ye Dark-elves down under—we call you! Fare ye forth from the realm and light upon the ray of the elves—stream to us from on high! Fare

ye forth from the realm of darkness upon the ray of elves—stream to us from down under!"

(5) *"We give this ale, blended with awe, to you wondrous wights of the land and airs, to you awesome elves all-old!"*

(7) *"This ale is hallowed to the elves of the kindred!"*
"To all the awesome elves, to those who dwell in darkness, and to those who live in light!"

(8) *"All ye elves of the elven realms,   Awesome elders all,*
                    Weird land-wights,
            To you we give this ale!"

(9) *"From these nights to the twelfth night of yule, the walls between the dwellings of those dark-elves and the light, and our world here, grow ever thinner—the lore of light and the dreams of darkness are becoming ever more known to us throughout this tide! Let us now go forth and make merry, for the year is yet but young!"*

The Greatest Blessing of the Yule-tide (December 20-31)

The Yule-tide is a complex blessing. Ideally it should be celebrated over the twelve nights between the Mother Night and the Twelfth Night (or Yule proper). During this time there should be general celebration among family and close friends. However, our modern world usually makes much of this impossible. Since the twelve nights of the Yule-tide represent the whole year, appropriate magical and divinatory workings can also effectively be undertaken during this time. It is fitting to read through the entire *Poetic Edda*, preferably out loud before the gathered folk in the evenings, during the twelve nights of the Yule-tide.

Mother-Night: Beginning of the Yule-Tide
(December 20)

On the Mother Night an all-around blessing is to be held, which will ritually be answered by the all-around blessing held at Midsummer. After the blessing the gathered folk will partake of the most important sumble of the year—the sumble of the Yule-tide, at which time the ancestors are naturally closest to us, the living.

The All-Around Blessing
of the Mother Night

The harrow is set up in the standard fashion.

1. Hallowing
The hammer-rite is performed, at the conclusion of which the speaker says:

"This stead is hallowed for our work here tonight. As the god Heimdall wards the Bifrost Bridge, so this stead is warded against all unholy wights and ways."

2. Reading (Lay)
The "Völuspá" and/or the "Lay of Helgi Hjorvarthsson" and the other "Helgi lays" are to be read or recited to the gathered folk.

3. Rede
The speaker says:

"This mid-night upon the mother night we gather together as in nights of yore, to greet the sun at her lowest stead, and to honor all the gods and goddesses who dwell in Asgard, and all our own forebears who dwell in the halls of Harr

and Hel. We call upon them to make ripe their might and
main in our lives. We call upon them all—the holy gathering—
living as a whole as is Woden's Law."

4. Call

The speaker makes the following calls. After each call,
the gathered folk give welcome to the god or goddess being
called with their name, and the words: *"We Give Thee
Welcome!"*

> *"Woden, we are awed by thy craft,*
> *Tiw, we stay true to thee forever,*
> *Balder, thy brightness and boldness guides us,*
> *Frigg, thy fruit and wisdom keeps us all,*
> *Idunna, thine apples strengthen our souls,*
> *Thunar, thy thunder wards our stead,*
> *Freya, we get freedom from thy frolic,*
> *Frey, from thee we get a harvest of Frith."*

Then a litany of divine attributes of the gods and goddesses just called is recited by the speaker. After each the
gathered folk shout: *"We give thee welcome!"*

> *"Rune-Lord,*
> *One-Handed God,*
> *Holder of the Hringhorn,*
> *Lady of the gods and goddesses,*
> *Keeper of the apples,*
> *Guardian of Asgard,*
> *Holder of the Brisingamen,*
> *God of the Wane."*

"Again we call to you in all your names, be among us here

*this mid-night as the year reaches its depth and sunna
stands at sunken to her lowest stead:*

> Hail all the gods,   Hail all the goddesses,
>   Hail all thy holy ones
>   Who dwell together!"

5. Loading

The speaker pours mead into the horn and says:

*"We give you the gifts of our works woven and blended
with the might and main of the mead. It lends us—gods
and folk together—help in our striving towards the
shining plain where the worlds and wights dwell in
wholeness. The year has come into its depth of darkness—the serpent slithers along the deepest roots of the
World Tree—may his sight find us not wanting in wisdom."*

6. Drinking

The speaker then drinks from the horn and pours the
remainder into the blessing bowl on the harrow. The horn
is then refilled and passed to each of the gathered folk.
Each makes the sign of the hammer over the rim of the horn
before drinking. Each time the remainder of the mead is
poured into the blessing bowl by the speaker.

7. Blessing

The speaker now sprinkles the harrow and the gathered
folk with the words:

*"The blessings of all the gods and all the goddesses of our
folk be upon us!"*

8. Giving

After the blessing is completed, the speaker pours the contents of the blessing bowl out upon the bare ground to the east of the harrow with the words:

"To Woden, Tiw, Balder, Frigga, Idunna, Thunar, Freya, Frey and to all the gods and goddesses of our folk: for good growth among folk and upon the land!"

9. Leaving

The speaker returns to the harrow and says:

"Thus the work is once again wrought, it renews our hearts to do worthy deeds, and to strive toward our goals with mighty moods, wise words, and trust in our own might and craft—ever holding our oaths to ourselves and to our folk!"

Twelfth Night: The Festival of Yule (December 31)

This is the culmination of the Yule-tide, and religiously the most important of the twelve nights of Yule. The rebirth of the Sun is completed on this night. In the deep tradition of the Yule-oath the origins of our "New Year's resolutions" are to be found.

The harrow, which must be made of stone and set up outside or in an indoor room with a chimney or smoke hole, is fitted out with the horn, a vessel of beer or ale, a single (red) candle and the Yule-wreath in its center.

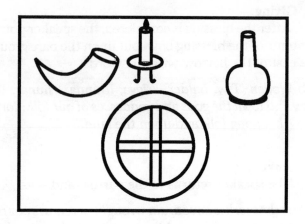

The Harrow

1. Hallowing

The stead is hallowed with the hammer-working, at the conclusion of which a ring is drawn on the ground around the gathered folk.

2. Call

The officiating speaker stands before the harrow, facing the north [ᛏ], and says:

> *"By the bristles of the boar!*
> *Jolnir (Woden) lord of the yule-tide*
> *We call upon thee to witness*
> *These our oaths of yule*
> *Jólaheit skaltu at heyra ok heit skullum vér at strengja!"*

("Thou shalt hear the oaths of Yule and we shall bind the oaths.")

3. Oath Taking

Each of the gathered true men and women, in order of rank and/or age, then steps up to the harrow and with the right hand grasps the center of the yule-wreath. With the left hand they lift the horn aloft and speak their own personal oath or boast. After the speech is through, he or she drinks half of the contents of the horn, and pours the rest out as a gift with the words:

"To Jolnir and to the oaths of Yule!"

As each person finishes, the officiating speaker refills the horn for the next one. This is repeated until all oaths are completed.

4. Lighting of the Yule-wreath

The speaker then takes up position before the harrow and pours out the holy fuel upon the Yule-wreath. This may be any hallowed flammable substance; rarefied butter or "ghee" is the most traditional. The pattern for pouring the fuel is:

As the speaker pours the fuel, he or she says:

> *"Jolnir, ruling the Yule-tide,*
> *We yearn for thy might,*
> *Yare the year in the yard to make!"*

Then from the flame of the red candle, signifying the old year passing away, the Yule-wreath is ignited, with the words:

> *"In the year of this Yule*
> *Are we tried and true:*
> *We plight our troth*
> *And truly pledge*
> *To hold these holy oaths*
> *In the year of this Yule!"*

As the wreath is burning, the speaker says:

> *"Jolnir, ruling the Yule,*
> *We yearn for thy might—*
> *That when the yarn of the year is yielded*
> *Yare the year in the yard was made!"*

The gathered folk then watch the flames as they burn the wreath, carrying their oaths aloft. While gazing at the embers of the wreath glowing on the harrow, individuals may be moved to make prophecies for the coming year.

5. Leaving

No formal closing is used here, as the purpose of the rite is the opening of the whole of the year to come. Each retreats in his or her own time back to the main gathering area.

The Great Blessing of Disting
(around February 14)

Disting is a festival of importance to the home region. It is given to the dises (from whom it gets its name), and thus it is strongly linked to the Winter Nights festival. But it is really given more for gatherings of a social and/or clanic nature, and traditionally at a time when local Things are held. At this time, the Earth is prepared to have the seeds sown so that growth will take place in the land.

If a formal Thing is held, the rites particular to opening and closing a Thing-stead should be performed. (These are described in detail in the section concerning the Tide of the Great Thing.) Also, gifts may be given to the dises and elves at this time. But the tide is really most holy to the goddess Freya and to the god Váli. Freya is very pronounced in her erotic aspect at this time, and blessings designed to bring out this quality are right to do during this tide. Also, it is the right time to do the Blessing of Váli, the god of vengeance, and thus of rebirth.

Blessing of Váli

For this working a piece of string or twine at least a foot long is needed.

1. Hallowing
Perform the hammer-working.

2. Reading
Read or recite the "Short Seeress Prophecy" from the *Poetic Edda*.

3. Rede
"On this day/night we remember the ties of kin, and understand our bonds with them. We remember as well our kindred oaths of troth and trust to the siblings gathered around the harrow."

4. Call
"Váli, son of Rind, the Etin-wife now among the Ases—and Sigtýr, son of Borr, born of Buri, spawn of the wind-cold corn!"

5. Loading
Mead, ale, or beer is poured into the horn. An assistant to the speaker stands with the twine held in a loose knot over the rim of the horn, as the speaker says:

"Dweller in the homesteads of the forebears—thou art the god who frees long-bound force! Unbind now the bond of narrow blindness—free us from the fetters in which we have long abode, apart from kith and kindred! Unbind the bonds and free the fetters—as the knot is un-knit . . . (here the knot over the rim of the horn is unknotted) *. . . boundless are the bonds, free are the fetters!*

Váli-Áli-Váli-Áli-Váli—god of vengeance—heave up the holy might of the old ones, who rest unquietly deep down below! Rebind us in their troth, again we hear their holy Rede, and with this knot we again know their mighty Myne!"

(Here the assistant ties twine onto the horn.)

> *"Váli to thee vows   and valued oaths*
> *Are gladly given   All great gifts:*
> *Lift the elders' lives   In love bind the kin*
> *In homes 'round holy hearths."*

(Speaker hallows the horn with the hammer-sign.)

6. Drinking

The Horn is passed around for each to hallow and drink from, and is returned to the speaker, who pours the remainder into the blessing bowl with the formula:

"Váli-Āli-Váli-Āli-Váli!"

7. Blessing

The holy liquid is sprinkled on the harrow and on the gathered folk with the words:

"May the blessings of Váli be upon this harrow and upon the gathered folk."

8. Giving

The holy liquid is poured out onto the ground to the west of the harrow with the words:

"To Váli, and to Freya, is this gift given!"

9. Leaving

"By the wonder of Woden, by the Troth of Tiw, and by the thunder of Thunar—so shall it be!"

The Greatest Blessing of Easter (Ostara): Spring Equinox (March 21)

This festival is traditionally celebrated with an all-night vigil, in which the gathered folk stay up throughout the night while remaining indoors. In the hour before sunrise, they make a procession to the area in which the blessing is to take place. This should ideally be where the sunrise can be clearly seen. As the first light of the spring is seen, the working begins.

The harrow is fitted out with a sword, horn, mead-vessel, blessing bowl, bough of evergreen, and three candles (black, red, and white), arranged in the following manner:

EAST

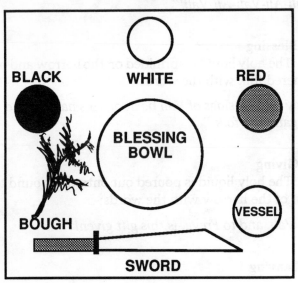

BLACK **WHITE** **RED**

BLESSING BOWL

VESSEL

BOUGH

SWORD

1. Hallowing

The hammer-working is performed.

The speaker faces the sunrise in the east in the [ᛉ] posture and says:

"This stead is hallowed to our work here this morning. As the god Heimdall wards the Bifrost Bridge, so the stead is warded aginst all unholy wights and ways."

After a pause the speaker continues:

"Hail holy Easter! Hail the daughter born at Delling's Door, at the Gate of Day who bears the light! Hail Easter, lady of the dawn!"

2. Reading

Here the "Sigrdrífumál" from the *Poetic Edda* is read or recited.

3. Rede

Still facing east, the speaker says:

"This morning we are gathered to call forth the mighty lady of the new-born light. Warded by the steeds of heaven, she rises and gives us light, love, and lust, and she bears also an awesome side, middling and mighty. This our foes shall doom, yet we too must know it well and love it well for to wax great in wisdom."

4. Call

Speaker raises sword from the harrow and salutes the east with the words:

"Easter, we raise the sign of the sword in thy honor, come and dwell among the folk of the Sax! In the dawn we see thy birth, in the day we know thy power, and in the dusk we trust that thou shalt turn back to us full well soon."

Speaker then replaces sword on the harrow and continues:

"No mask has hidden thy holy name from us, and now we call thee forth by deeds right and holy:
Easter—drottning of the dawn, queen of heaven—clothed in white and gold—break now forth in all thy might, let us know thy main!"

The speaker now lights the three candles on the altar in the order: white, red, black. As he or she lights them, the following is spoken:

"We now kindle the three-fold fire of spring, in this new dawn of the year we start the fire of its birth (white candle

is lit), *we light the flame of its life* (red candle is lit), *and we kindle the lamp of its death* (black candle is lit)—*as signs of the timeless, ever-becoming power in our souls."*

5. Loading
Speaker pours mead into the horn and holds it aloft with the words:

"To thee, awesome Easter, who knows the ways of Woden, we give to thee the gifts of our works all woven and blended with the might of this mead. As we lend you this mead, so lend us thy might—haunt our hearts, abide in our breaths, make whole our minds and mighty our moods and memories!

Hail Easter!
Hail the awesome Ostara! Ostara! Ostara!"

6. Drinking
The horn is then passed among the gathered folk and the remainder is poured into the blessing bowl on the harrow by the speaker.

7. Blessing
The speaker then goes on to sprinkle first the harrow (turning around it three times with the sun), and then all the good folk and true. While doing this the speaker repeats at will:

"The blessings of Easter upon us!"

8. Giving
The speaker then pours out the contents of the blessing bowl to the east of the harrow with the words:

"To Easter we give this gift!"

9. Leaving

The blessing bowl is returned to the harrow, the speaker faces the new dawn and says:

"Thus is the work of wonder wrought! The fires of spring burn, the power of Easter burns forth, she blooms in our minds, and we move with her might. We know her blessings all the year through!"

At the conclusion of the working it is traditional to leap up in the air as high as you can three times. Also, there is the tradition of tossing an Easter-egg high into the air and catching it. If this operation is successful, it is a good omen for things to come in the year. Such eggs, or their shells, are powerful charms.

The Great Blessings of Walburga and May-Day
The Festival of Walburga's Night (April 30) and May-Day (May 1)

Walburga's Night

Walburga's Night is the most mysterious of the rites normally performed by an all-around kindred or hearth. It contains many runic (secret) elements (most find it very beneficial to delve into the depths of the self on occasion). The working formula is slightly different from the other blessings. It is sharply contrasted with the bright, life-bearing festivities of the following day.

The harrow is set up in the following fashion, with a fire pit to the south of it. The diagram also indicates the directions for the dance around the fire described in the Yielding section below.

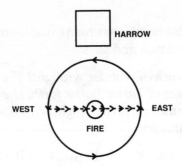

1. Hallowing

All stand in a half-circle in the south, facing the north around the harrow, and the speaker says:

"The Hof is about to be raised on high—let all within this Hof and about this harrow be here of their own free will and in full Frith and Grith."

The speaker then places the point of the knife in a vessel containing a mixture of salt and yeast, and says:

"Salt and yeast are the seeds of life. Now are this salt and this yeast hallowed, and they shall make holy our lives, as we wield them in these works of craft given to Woden and Freya."

Water is now poured into the salt-yeast mixture, and the speaker stirs them together with the point of the knife, saying:

"The holy salt drives out any ill in this water and the yeast quickens it—together they may be wielded in the worship of Woden and Freya, throughout these workings."

The solution of water, yeast, and salt is then poured in a ring around the harrow, as the speaker says:

"Woden and Freya, god and goddess, father and mother of

all might and main, here do we call upon you to come together with us in our workings. Ward us well and steer us within this ring and without it. So shall it be!"

To which all respond:

"So shall it be."

2. Reading (optional)
Read or recite the "Lokasenna" from the *Poetic Edda*.

3. The Loading
The speaker faces north in the [ᛉ] and says:

"Upon this night we see the ending of the dark tide—our lord Galster-Father has gone through to bring us once more to the light of lady Freya, the fair. Here we stand at midnight with the might of the Moon on the wane and that of sunna waxing—in the twixt and twain shall we see the inner light of day!"

The center fire pit is now ignited, while the speaker says:

"Now we light the beacon of Walburga to quicken the might of life and of our inner sight on its long road-wending!

> *Welcome Woden!*   [all repeat]
> *Welcome Walburga!"*   [all repeat]

The speaker, still facing north, says:

"Out of the horns of heaven all-eight we call upon you ever-living ones—come ye elder queens, ye ides from out of the airts—drive out of the airts O drighten of dread to us to work thy wonders—fare now forth Walburga, wish-wife of a hundred wonders—ward our way down below and

steer us on the nether roads to inner sight!
The Ides are among us!   [all repeat]
Woden is with us!   [all repeat]
Walburga and Freya wile are among us!" [all repeat]

5. Yielding

The speaker turns to face the gathered folk and says:

"Now the loke and play along thy road begins O mighty one within the ring of the staff!"

The gathered folk begin to dance around the central fire pit in a widdershins (counterclockwise) direction. Those who wish to may break through the ring in a west-to-east direction to jump over the central fire pit. This is done to gain inner vision and a quickening of life.

During the dance, the officiating speaker performs the Blessing of Walburga. The speaker pours ale into the horn and says:

"To thee O Walburga—in memory of the gore of the goat! Take well with this our gift to thee!"

The speaker then pours the ale down the "gift hole" that has been drilled into the Earth to the north of the harrow.

The dance continues until all have been touched by Walburga, whereupon they sit in a half-circle to the north of the harrow facing the fire. When all are in a meditative state, the speaker says:

"We all have wended our way to Walburga—let us see her wonders!"

All meditate on the fire and the horn is passed around once in total silence. The remainder of the ale is poured into the gift-hole.

6. Closing

The speaker goes to the harrow and says:

"Now the work has been wrought—let us now go to sumble to share our gifts with Walburga, with the ides, and with their queen, Freya!"

7. Sumble

The horn is passed around once, with a full given by each of the gathered folk who wishes to do so. Then the horn is retired to the harrow to be used at will throughout the sumble.

May Day

On the following day, May First, general festivities are held celebrating the Spring-tide and the playful aspects of life. There need be no blessings or other workings. However, it is sometimes the practice to set up the 'May-Pole' at this time. The other, more usual, option is to set up the May-Pole at the Midsummer-tide.

The Greatest Blessing of Midsummer (June 21)

This is one of the three Greatest Blessings of the Troth, at which gifts are yielded to all of the gods and goddesses of the Troth together. The celebration of these three blessings, the other two being Yule and Harvest, are the essential acts of good and true men and women.

The harrow is set up in the standard fashion.

1. Hallowing

The hammer-rite is performed, at the conclusion of which the speaker says:

"This stead is hallowed for our work here today. As the god Heimdall wards the Bifrost Bridge, so this stead is warded against all unholy wights and ways."

2. Reading (Lay)

The lay of "Baldr's Dreams" is read or recited to the gathered folk.

3. Rede

The speaker says:

"This noon-tide of the midsummer we gather together as in days of Yore, to greet the sun at her highest stead, and to honor all the gods and goddesses who dwell in Asgard. We call upon them to make ripe their might and main in our lives. We call upon them all—the holy many—living as a whole as is Woden's law."

4. Call

The speaker makes the following calls. After each call, the gathered folk give welcome to the god or goddess being called with their name, and add the words: *"We give thee welcome!"*

> *"Woden, we are awed by thy craft,*
> *Tiw, we stay true to thee forever,*
> *Balder, thy brightness and boldness guides us,*
> *Frigg, thy fruit and wisdom keeps us all,*
> *Idunna, thine apples ward our ways,*
> *Thunar, thy thunder wards our stead,*
> *Freya, we get freedom from thy frolic,*
> *Frey, from thee we get a harvest of Frith."*

Then a litany of divine attributes of the gods and goddesses just called is recited by the speaker. After each the gathered folk shout: *"We give thee welcome!"*

> *"Rune-Lord,*
> *One-handed God,*
> *Holder of the Hringhorn,*
> *Lady of the gods and goddesses,*
> *Keeper of the Apples,*
> *Guardian of Asgard,*
> *Holder of the Brisingamen,*
> *God of the Wane.*

Again we call to you in all your names, be among us here this noon-tide as the year reaches its height and Sunna stands at her strongest stead:

> *Hail all the gods,   Hail all the goddesses,*
> *Hail all thy holy ones*
> *Who dwell together!"*

5. Loading

The speaker pours mead into the horn, lifts its aloft, and says:

"We give you the gifts of our works woven and blended with the might and main of the mead. It lends us—gods and folk together—help in our striving towards the shining plain where the worlds and wights dwell in wholeness. The year has come to its peak of power—the eagle gazes from the topmost branch of the world tree—may his sight find us not wanting in wisdom."

6. Drinking

The speaker then drinks from the horn and pours the remainder into the blessing bowl on the harrow. The horn is then refilled and passed to each of the gathered folk. Each makes the sign of the hammer over the rim of the horn before drinking. Each time the remainder of the mead is poured into the blessing bowl by the speaker.

7. Blessing

The speaker now sprinkles the harrow and the gathered folk with the words:

"The blessings of all the gods and all the goddesses of our folk be upon us!"

8. Giving

After the blessing is completed, the speaker pours the contents of the blessing bowl out upon the bare ground to the east of the harrow with the words:

"To Woden, Tiw, Balder, Frigg, Idunna, Thunar, Freya, Frey and to all the gods and goddesses of our folk: for good harvest and Frith!"

9. Leaving

The speaker returns to the harrow and says:

"Thus the work is once again wrought. It renews our hearts to do worthy deeds, and to strive toward our goals with mighty moods, wise words, and trust in our own powers— ever holding our oaths to ourselves and to our folk!"

The Great Blessing of the Thing's Tide (around August 23)

The Thing is a very complex institution. It is a political convention, a session of government, a court of law, a religious festival, a fair or market, and a party, all wrapped into one. Its timing is also interesting. It comes in late summer (for northern climes) and should be called to begin in the three or four days leading up to a Full Moon.

Religiously, the high point of the Thing-Tide should be the performance of an all-around blessing to all the gods and goddesses, like the ones performed at Yule or Midsummer. The Thing-Tide is called to order with a Blessing of Tiw on the evening of the first day of the Thing, and is called to an end with another Blessing of Tiw on the morning of the last day.

A Blessing of Tiw

1. Hallowing

The hammer-working is done, and then the speaker says:

"This thing–stead is hallowed for our work here all these days and nights. By the hammer of Thunar is it warded against all that would work ill against us. May we meet in Frith and take leave in Grith."

2. Reading

The section of the *Prose Edda* dealing with the loss of Týr's hand to the Fenris-Wolf is read or recited.

3. Rede

"Under the might and main of the great god Tiw, we are gathered together here, gods and folk together, to hold a holy thing. May he make our moods all-mighty and our words all-wise."

4. Call

"From thy stead deep within the Yrminsul we call to thee O mighty lord of laws and leavings of the wolf! Thou who,

*by the ordeal of battle, metes out good speed and bad, in
the highest of laws all-whole. Fare now forth, O mighty
one-handed god from thy high-seat deep within the most
hidden halls of Asgard! Come shine thy light of law and
right over our deeds and doings upon this thing-stead!"*

5. Loading
The speaker pours mead into the horn, lifts it aloft,
and says:

*"We give you this horn blended with the might and main of
all our deeds and doings, that thou shalt mete out that law
as we all have it coming to us! Tiw! Tiw!"*

6. Drinking
The speaker makes the sign of the hammer over the
rim of the horn, drinks from it, and passes it around to the
gathered folk; all make the sign of the hammer or that of
the T-rune before drinking. The remainder of the mead in
the horn is poured into the blessing bowl on the harrow.

7. Blessing
The speaker turns twice around the harrow, sprinkling
it with the mead, while saying:

"The great blessing of Tiw be upon this thing-stead!"

Then the speaker sprinkles the gathered folk, saying:

"And may his blessing be upon all the gathered folk!"

8. Giving
The blessing bowl is poured out to the north of the
harrow with the words:

*"To Tiw, high-god of the heavens, and to Earth, mother of
us all!"*

9. Leaving

"Thus our work is wrought. Let us now go forth and speak with wise words, make law with mighty moods, hold hard to our oaths of Troth and fellowship, and make merry in Frith and Grith!"

The Harvest Festival
The Greater Blessing of the Wanes
(Autumnal Equinox: September 23)

The harrow is set up in the usual way, with the addition of an antler, as shown in the diagram below.

1. Hallowing

The hammer-rite is performed, at the conclusion of which the speaker says:

"Wise Wanes and mighty, who ever wend your ways through the world and shower blessings upon your kindred here on the Earth—mother of us all!"

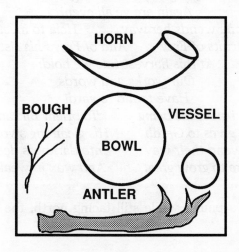

2. Reading

The "Skírnismál" is now read or recited.

3. Rede

"Now is come the tide of the harvest of our deeds—all that we have wrought is come again to us as our right reward. Let us now give thanks to the gods and goddesses among the wanes in whose bounties we abide."

4. Call

The speaker faces north with the antler horn held aloft and says:

"We hear you in the rustling leaves of fall—in the harvest ham we smell you—we taste you on our lovers' lips—in the crops newly cut we see you—we feel you in the winds of the coming winter.

Hail thee day!   Hail the sons of day!
Hail night and her daughters!
Again are ye all even!
Sunna wends her way   Hela to meet.
The fruits of Frey   And of Freya his sister,
At this harvest tide we hold:
Our works and words
Have found reward!
Ingvi gives his being   To bright Birkana
Frey gives to Gerdh   His gleaming sword
All wend their way   Into darkness deep
There to grow great   And wax in weal!"

After a pause, while still facing north, the speaker says:

"We call upon you Wanes all-mighty! Come and witness our work and ward our ways! Be now among us, that we may give freely our holy gifts."

The speaker now turns to the east and holds out the antler and says:

"From the east we call Freya!"

                (Response: *"Freya is with us!"*)

Speaker then turns to the southeast and says:

"From the inner-south we call Vaningi!"

                (Response: *"Vaningi is with us!"*)

Speaker now turns to the south and says:

"From the South we call Birkana!"

                (Response: *"Birkana is with us!"*)

Speaker then turns to the southwest and says:

"From the outer-south we call Vanadis!"

                (Response: *"Vanadis is with us!"*)

Speaker then turns to the west and says:

"From the west we call Frey!"

                (Response: *"Frey is with us!"*)

Speaker then turns to the northwest and says:

"From the outer-north we call Skírnir!"

                (Response: *"Skírnir is with us!"*)

Speaker then turns to the north and says:

"From the north we call Ingvi!"

                (Response: *"Ingvi is with us!"*)

Speaker then turns to the northeast and says:

"From the inner-north we call Gerdh!"

                (Response: *"Gerdh is with us!"*)

5. Loading

The speaker then returns to a position in front of the harrow, pours the mead into the drinking horn, and holds it aloft, saying:

"We give the gifts of our deeds and doings, betokened by this mead—all blended with might and main. May this gift be given back to us anew, that we may work with our kindred wights and realms all-round—toward ever greater growth and weal!"

6. Drinking

After making the sign of the hammer over the rim of the horn, the speaker drinks some of the mead and pours what remains in the horn into the blessing bowl. The horn is then passed around to the gathered folk and what remains is then poured into the blessing bowl.

7. Blessing

The speaker now takes up the evergreen bough and sprinkles the harrow, turning around it three times with the sun, while saying:

"I hallow the harrow with the blood of Kvasir!"

Then the speaker turns outward and blesses the eight corners of heaven (the eight directions). The whole time the speaker is doing this, he or she repeats:

"I hallow all the horns of heaven with Kvasir's blood!"

Finally each of the true men and women present is blessed. All the while the speaker is doing this, he or she repeats:

"The blessings of the holy wanes be upon you all!"

8. Giving

The speaker then returns to the harrow and takes up the blessing bowl, carrying it to a point just west of the harrow. There the mead is poured out with the words:

"Take well with this our gift to you O mighty Wanes in the west!"

9. Leaving

Facing the harrow, the speaker says:

"The gifts of harvest have been given, and we have gotten our right rewards this year. Now let us again go forward, gathering new and great deeds and doings, that next year's harvest shall be greater still! Now, we wend our way, to sit at ale with the holy gods and goddesses gathered with us tonight. Thus the work by the harrow is wrought!"

Part III
The Troth

31

The Troth and the Ring of Troth

There are essentially two levels of the Troth. The first is the folk-troth. This to some extent could be considered as all people in the Ásatrú/Odinist movement in general, organized or unorganized, in the English speaking world who would generally hold to the basic tenets outlined in the pages of this book, whether or not its members would agree with or hold to every word. But in a slightly more formal way, the Troth at this level is made up of all those true men and women who have joined the Ring of Troth, and therefore have the right to wear the Troth-Hammer as a token of their own troth. These true folk can form kindreds as they will, and according to their own custom, outside the rules and regulations of the Ring of Troth. By simply affiliating with the Troth, and following the general outlines of this book together with the important source works of the Troth, anyone can belong to the good folk and true.

The other level of the Troth is the more formal one. This is the Ring of Troth—the formal organization sometimes also simply called the Troth. It is governed by strict legal standards established by the High Rede of Troth, which is the "board of directors" for the Ring of Troth. The main function of the Ring of Troth is to oversee the whole of the movement in a spiritual way. In practical terms this involves three main tasks: 1) the setting of a training curriculum for Elders of the Troth; 2) the ritual ordination or naming of Elders of the Troth; and 3) the licensing of the Elders (which enables any one of them to establish a local Hof). The main spiritual value of this lies in the fact that when someone is a true Elder within the Ring of Troth, it will be a matter of public record as to what training that person has had, and what qualifications he or she has for being called a Troth-Elder. Troth-Elders are subject to internal reviews and ethical standards, as well as, and more importantly, continuing standards of knowledge and work. In short, the Ring of Troth exists to re-establish a true "priesthood" within our folk.

The Elders of the Troth may or may not be salaried workers within the Ring of Troth. They also have the right to set up licensed hofs, from which income may be generated through hof-tolls, or donations from the local folk. This is up to the individual Elder and the folk he or she works with, but this is with the responsibilities of their work.

What is imperative for us to realize at this point in our history is that we need highly trained men and women working full-time at the restoration of the Troth. Part-time priests will only get part-time results. We have no more time for partial results. Some have objected that there were no professional priests in the ancient North. In the first place, this is not true; but more to the point it is important to realize that in ancient times, when the Troth was the *established* religion, people who already owned the land and the means of production were its priests and priestesses, or were represented by them. Additionally, they had thousands of years *behind* them, propelling them forward; they had only to maintain the momentum. We have a thousand years of history on top of us, weighing us down. It will take a heroic effort on the parts of many men and women to heave this weight from us. When the size of the task is fully understood, the nature of the work should be obvious, and any such objections to men and women working full-time to restore our Troth will be withdrawn.

The High Rede of Troth is the governing board of the Ring of Troth. It consists of eight members plus a ninth member who coordinates and leads the Rede. All members of the High Rede must be Troth-Elders or their equal. In addition there is a steersman, who is responsible for the day-in, day-out running of the Ring of Troth.

Local Troth organizations are of several sorts: the kindred, the hearth, the garth, and the hof. The kindred is a group of true folk who may or may not be members of the Ring of Troth, but who are true.

Kindreds may be formed by anyone without approval by the Ring of Troth. This would also include individual true men and women working alone. The other three kinds of local organizations may only be formed officially after word has been received from the High Rede of the Ring of Troth.

The hearth is made up of a group of two or more members of the Ring of Troth. One of these will be elected hearth leader. A hearth may also be a family or group of families dedicated to the gods and goddesses. The garth is also a group of two or more, led by a Troth-Elder or by a man or woman officially training to become a Troth-Elder. Both the hearth and the garth usually meet in the homes of the members, or in other faculties secured for the purpose of meeting or holding blessings. The hof is not only a group of folk, but also a piece of land or property belonging to the Ring of Troth and overseen by a Troth-Elder. It is a holy stead given to the gods and goddesses of our Troth. The hof may be seen as analogous to the church of the Christians. It is a permanent local site where a Troth-Elder regularly holds the blessings. Members of the Ring of Troth further affiliate with these local hofs, and become members of them in addition to their affiliation with the Ring of Troth.

The activities of these various levels of organization are for the most part determined by the members themselves. The one set of obligations that all hofs and Troth-Elders have in common is that they must work the Great Blessings of the Year and hold regular talks on the character of the Troth for members and prospective members alike.

All persons interested in affiliating with the Ring of Troth are urged to write to the Troth at the address provided on page 211 of this book.

32

Becoming a Troth-Elder

At various points in this book reference has been made to the "priesthood" of the Ring of Troth. Members of this body are called Troth-Elders. In some forms of the Ásatrú/Odinist movement the "priesthood" is referred to by the Old Norse terms *godhi* (for men) and *gydhja* (for women). We do not often use Old Norse terms in the Troth simply because we do not feel the need to resort to exotic forms to express our own folk-troth.

When someone is called a Troth-Elder, it means certain things. It means that the person has undergone a rigorous training in the heart and lore of the folk and that they have met a set of other criteria established by the High Rede which qualify them to represent the Ring of Troth in an official capacity. Elders are licensed, ceremonially named to their office by the High Rede, and have the right to set up a hof in a local area, or to undertake other official work for the Ring of Troth.

Here we would briefly like to outline just what it means to become a Troth-Elder, and what the basic qualifications are. This will serve two purposes: first, for those interested in becoming Troth-Elders, you will be able to see what kind of work you have cut out for yourself. Also, those who may in the future come into contact with Troth-Elders will know what kind of training the elders have undergone, and what qualifications they have which enable them to be known as Troth-Elders.

The qualifications to become a Troth-Elder are in some ways flexible, but in other regards they are firmly set. This is to recognize the fact that every individual has different talents and areas of special interest, while at the same time ensuring that a basic and high level of knowledge and ability is signified by the title Troth-Elder.

The qualifications to become a Troth-Elder

1. The candidate must be at least twenty-five years of age.
2. The candidate must have had an official affiliation with the Ring of Troth for at least five years prior to the date of his or her prospective naming as an Elder.
3. The candidate must be maintaining an independent lifestyle, that is, he or she must be financially self-supporting.
4. The candidate must have a record of at least two years leading a Hearth or Garth and of conducting and/or leading the working of the Great Blessings of the Year.
5. The candidate must have a degree from an accredited institution of higher learning in a field related to his or her work in the Troth. (A degree in Teutonic studies is ideal; inappropriate would be things such as chemistry, engineering, etc.)
6. The candidate must submit a written work on some specialized topic within the Troth. This topic must have prior approval by the High Rede and the final work must meet with the standards of quality established by the High Rede.

7. The candidate must complete a written exam on matters of basic lore and history relevant to the Troth.
8. The candidate must pass on the basis of an oral interview before two or more members of the High Rede or their designated representatives.
9. The candidate must be ceremonially installed and named as a Troth-Elder in a working attended by at least one member of the High Rede of Troth.

Once these nine criteria are met, one can be called a Troth-Elder good and true.

Of all of the qualifications shown above, the fifth one, requiring a university degree, will perhaps be seen by some to be out of place. So perhaps a further word of explanation is in order. In many major universities around the country, great storehouses of learning and lore concerning our folk and troth are to be found. This has all been "secularized" to be sure, but that is how it has been protected and continued. The latest developments along the lines of inquiry begun by the Romantics of the late 1700s and early 1800s are now to be found there. With this requirement, the High Rede incorporates and co-opts the institutions of higher learning to our own purposes. This is just a further extension of the journeyman process. In addition to the lore that will be learned, the completion of such a degree, especially one beyond the B.A. level, will be a token of one's ability to see an endeavor through to its end—sometimes under adverse conditions.

More detailed information on the process of becoming a Troth-Elder, and how previous work and works can be applied toward that end, can also be obtained from the High Rede at the address printed on page 211.

For further information on the Troth write:
The Ring of Troth
P.O. Box 18812
Austin, Texas 78760

For information on runic practice write:
The Rune-Gild
P.O. Box 7622
Austin, TX 78713

Glossary

This glossary of technical words used throughout the text of this book indicates the exact definitions of words that might be used in unfamiliar contexts. Here the Old English (OE) or Old Norse (ON) terms from which some of these technical terms are ultimately derived are also provided.

Ase, pl. *Ases* [pron. 'ace']: The gods and goddesses of consciousness in the Teutonic pantheon, governing the powers of sovereignty and physical force (ON *Ass*; *Æsir*).

Asgard: The enclosure of the gods, the realm where the gods and goddesses exist. (ON *Asgardhr*)

athem: The 'breath of life,' the vital force of life borne in the breath (OE *æthm*).

blessing: The act of sacrificing and distributing the powers of the gods and goddesses in Midgard (OE *blotan,* and *bletsian,* to sacrifice).

boast: A ritual drinking to the honor of a god, goddess, or ancestor, or drinking to seal an oath for future actions. Also, a "toast" (OE *beot*).

call: The part of a ritual in which the divine forces to take part in the blessing are invoked.

drinking: The part of a ritual in which the liquid charged with the divine forces is ingested by the gathered folk.

earth: 1) The natural, physical aspects of the universe; 2) The planet Earth; 3) Soil.

Elder: A recognized "priest" or "priestess" in the Ring of Troth (OE *ealdor*).

folk: 1) The Teutonic nation (all people of Teutonic heritage); 2) The people gathered for a holy event.

giving: The part of a ritual in which the remainder of the charged liquid not consumed by the gathered folk is returned to the divine realm. Also called the "yielding."

goodman: In a ritual in which active roles are divided, this is the one most responsible for the ritual actions and manipulations of the sacred objects (OE *godman*).

hallowing: The part of a ritual in which the space in which the ritual is to be performed is marked off from the profane world, made holy, and protected.

harrow: 1) An outdoor altar usually made of stone; 2) A general term for the altar in a true working (OE *hearg*).

holy: There are two aspects to this term: 1) that which is filled with divine power, and 2) that which is marked off and separate from the profane.

hugh: The cognitive part of the soul, the intellect or mind. Also called 'hidge' (OE *hyge*).

leaving: The formal closing of a ritual.

loading: The part of a ritual in which the sacred power that has been called upon is channeled into the holy drink.

lore: The tradition in all its aspects.

lyke: The physical part of the soul-body (psychophysical) complex. Also called 'lich' (OE *lic*).

Midgard: The dwelling place of humanity, the physical plane of existence. Also, Mid-Yard, the enclosure in the midst of all (OE *Middangeard*). Meddlert.

myne: The reflective part of the soul, the memory: personal and transpersonal (OE *mynd*, ON *minni*).

nightly: Sometimes used instead of "daily."

reading: The part of a ritual in which a mythic-poetic

text is recited in order to place the gathering into a mythic time/space, to engage in the mythic flow of timelessness.

rede: The part of a ritual in which the purpose for the working is stated.

shope: In a ritual in which the active roles are divided, this is the one most responsible for the speaking of the words designed to set the mythic and social context (OE *scop*).

soul: 1) A general term for the psychic parts of the psycho-physical complex; 2) The postmortem shade (OE *saw*).

stall: An indoor altar, especially one that is backed up against an interior wall (ON *stalli*).

sumble: The sacred ritual feast at which boasts are drunk (OE *symble*).

theal: In a ritual in which active roles are divided, this is the one most responsible for the speaking of the words designed to engage the mythic and divine powers (OE *thyle*).

tide: A time, occasion; a span of time with a definite beginning and end.

troth: Religion, being loyal to the gods, goddesses and cultural values of the ancestors (ON *trú*, OE *treowth*).

true: Adjective form of "troth," can mean "loyal." A "true man" is a man loyal to the gods and goddesses of his ancestors.

Wane, pl. Wanes: The gods and goddesses of organic existence in the Teutonic pantheon, governing the realms of organic production, eroticism, wealth, and physical well-being (ON *Van; Vanir*).

world: The psycho-chronic human aspects of the manifested universe (OE *weoruld*, the age of a man). The cosmos.

wyrd: The process of the unseen web of synchronicity and cause and effect throughout the cosmos. Weird.

Bibliography

The works cited here are valuable source books for further work in the development of the Troth. In many ways, this work represents a synthesis of their contents.

Askeberg, Fritz. *Norden och kontinenten i gammeltid. Studier in forngermansk kulturhistoria.* Uppsala: Almqvist & Wiksell, 1944.

Auld, Richard L. "The Psychological and Mythic Unity of the God Odhinn." *Numen*, 23:2 (1976), 145-160.

Baetke, Walter. *Das Heilige im Germanischen.* Tübingen: Mohr, 1942.

Barlau, Stephen. "Germanic Kinship." Diss. University of Texas at Austin, 1975.

Bauschatz, Paul C. "The Germanic Ritual Feast." In: *The Nordic Languages and Modern Linguistics 3*, Ed. John M. Weinstock. Austin: University of Texas Press, 1976, 289-294.

_____. *The Well and the Tree: World and Time in Early Germanic Culture.* Amherst: University of Massachusetts Press, 1982.

Benveniste, Emil. *Indo-European Language and Society*, tr. E. Palmer. Coral Gables, FL: University of Miami Press, 1973.

Berkeli, Emil. *Fedrekult in Norge. Et forsøk på en system-atisk-deskriptiv fremsteilling*. Oslo: Dybwad, 1938.

Binterim, Anton Joseph. *Von dem Aberglauben der deutschen Christen im Mittelalter*, ed. M Ach. Munich: Arbeits-gemeinschaft für Religions- und Weltanschauungs-fragen, 1977.

Bosworth, Joseph and T. Northcote Toller. *An Anglo-Saxon Dictionary*. Oxford: Oxford University Press, 1898.

Branston, Brian. *Gods of the North*. London: Thames & Hudson, 1955.

_____. *The Lost Gods of England*. London: Thames & Hudson, 1957.

Buchholz, Peter. "Schamanistische Züge in der altislan-dischen Überlieferung." Diss. Münster, 1968.

Caesar, Julius. *Commentarii de Bello Gallico*. Erklärt von Friedrich Kraner und W. Dittenberger. Berlin: Weid-mann, 1961. 3 vols.

Campbell, Joseph. *The Hero with a Thousand Faces*. (Bol-lingen Series 17). Princeton: Princeton University Press, 1949.

Chadwick, H. M. *The Cult of Othin*. London: Clay, 1899.

Chaney, William A. *The Cult of Kingship in Anglo-Saxon England*. Berkeley: University of California Press, 1970.

Chisholm, James A. *The Grove and the Gallows: Germanic Heathenism in the Greek and Latin Sources*. Austin: The Rune-Gild, 1987.

Cleasby, Richard and Gudbrand Vigfusson. *An Icelandic-English Dictionary*. Oxford: Oxford University Press, 1957.

Clemen, Carl. *Fontes historiae religionis Germanicae*. Berlin: de Gruyter, 1928.

Davidson, Hilda R. (Ellis). *The Road to Hel*. Cambridge: Cambridge University Press, 1943.

_____. *Gods and Myths of Northern Europe*. Har-mondsworth: Penguin, 1964.

Dumézil, Georges. *The Destiny of the Warrior*, tr. A. Hiltebeitel. Chicago: University of Chicago Press, 1970.

_____. *From Myth to Fiction: The Saga of Hadingus*, tr. D. Coltman. Chicago: University of Chicago Press, 1973.

_____. *Gods of the Ancient Northmen*, E. Haugen, ed. Berkeley: University of California Press, 1973.

Düwel, Klaus. "Das Opferfest von Lade and die Geschichte vom Volsi." Habilitation, Göttingen, 1971.

Eckhardt, Karl August. *Irdische Unsterblichkeit: Germanischer Glaube an die Wiederverkorperung in der Sippe*. Weimar: Bohlaus, 1937.

Einarson, Stefan. *A History of Icelandic Literature*. New York: Johns Hopkins Press, 1957.

Elliott, Ralph. *Runes: An Introduction*. Manchester: Manchester University Press, 1959.

Eliade, Mircea. *Rites and Symbols of Initiation: The Mysteries of Birth and Re-birth*, tr. W. R. Trask. New York: Harper & Row, 1958.

_____. *The Myth of the Eternal Return, or Cosmos and History*, tr. W. R. Trask. (Bollingen Series 46). Princeton: Princeton University Press, 1971.

_____. *Shamanism: Archaic Techniques of Ecstasy*, tr. W.R. Trask. (Bollingen Series 76). Princeton: Princeton University Press, 1972.

_____. *A History of Religious Ideas*. Chicago: University of Chicago Press, 1978-85, 3 vols.

Falk, Hjalmar. *Odensheite*. Kristiana: Dybwad, 1924.

_____. "Sjelen i Hedentoen." *Maal og Minne* 1926, pp. 169-174.

Finch, R.G. *The Saga of the Volsungs*. London: Nelson, 1965.

Fleck, Jere. "Konr-Ottarr-Geirodhr: A Knowledge Criterion for Succession to the Germanic Sacred Kingship."

Scandinavian Studies, 42 (1970), pp. 39-49.

————. "Odhinn's Self-Sacrifice—A New Interpretation: I/The Ritual Inversion." *Scandinavian Studies*, 43:2 (1971), pp. 119-142.

————. "Odhinn's Self-Sacrifice—A New Interpretation: II/The Ritual Landscape." *Scandinavian Studies*, 43:4 (1971), pp. 385-413.

————. "The Knowledge Criterion in the Grimnismal: The Case Against Shamanism." *Arkiv for Nordisk Filologi*, 86 (1971), pp. 49-65.

Flowers, Stephen E. "Revival of Germanic Religion in Contemporary Anglo-American Culture." *Mankind Quarterly*, 21:3 (1981), pp. 279-294.

————. "Toward an Archaic Germanic Psychology." *Journal of Indo-European Studies*, 11:1-2 (1983), pp. 117-138.

————. *Sigurdr, Rebirth and Initiation*. Austin: The Rune-Gild, 1985.

————. *Runes and Magic: Magical Formulaic Elements in the Older Runic Tradition*. New York: Lang, 1986.

————, ed. *The Galdrabok: A Medieval Icelandic Grimoire*. York Beach, ME: Weiser, 1989.

Gennep, Arnold van. *The Rites of Passage*, tr. M.B. Vizedom & G.L. Caffeee. Chicago: University of Chicago Press, 1960.

Golther, Wolfgang. *Handbuch der germanischen Mythologie*. Leipzig: Hirzel, 1895.

Grimm, Jacob. *Teutonic Mythology*, tr. S. Stallybrass. New York: Dover, 1966, 4 vols.

Grønbech, Vilhelm. *The Culture of the Teutons*. London: Oxford University Press, 1931, 2 vols.

Gruber, Loren C. "The Rites of Passage: Hávamál Stanzas 1-5." *Scandinavian Studies*, 49:3 (1977), pp. 330-340.

Harbard, Sigi (pseud.). *The New Odinism*. Woodland Hills, CA: Asgard Enterprises, 1982.

Helm, Karl. "Altgermanaische Religion." In: *Germanische Wiedererstehung*, ed. H. Nollau. Heidelberg: Winter, 1926.

————. *Altgermanische Religionsgeschichte: Die Ostgermanen*. Hiedelberg: Winter, 1937, Vol. II, part. 1.

————. *Altgermanische Religionsgeschichte: Die Westgermanen*. Heidelberg: Winter, 1953, Vol. II, part. 2.

Hempel, Heinrich, "Matronenkult und germanischer Mutterglaube." *Germanisch-romanische Monatsschrift*, 27 (1939), pp. 245-270.

Hermann, Paul. *Nordische Mythologie*. Leipzig: Engelmann, 1903.

Heusler, Andreas. *Das Strafrecht der Isländersagas*. Leipzig: Duncker & Humbolt, 1911.

Höfler, Otto. *Kultische Geheimbunde der Germanen*. Frankfurt/Main: Diesterweg, 1934.

————. *Germanisches Sakralkönigtum*. Tubingen: Niemeyer, 1952.

————. "Abstammungstraditionen." *Reallexikon der germanischen Altertumskunde* 1:1 (1973), pp. 18-29.

Hollander, Lee M., tr. *The Poetic Edda*. Austin: University of Texas Press, 1962, 2nd. ed.

Ingham, Marion. *The Goddess Freyja and Other Female Figures in Germanic Mythology and Folklore*. Ann Arbor, MI: University Microfilms, 1985.

Jones, Gwyn. *A History of the Vikings*. London: Oxford University Press, 1968.

Jonsson, Finnur, ed. *Den Norsk-Islandske Skjaldedigtning*. Copenhagen: Gyldendal, 1908, 2 vols.

Jonsson, Gudhni. *Islendinga Sogur*. Reykjavik: Islendingasagnautgafan, 1949, 13 vols.

————. *Fornaldarsögur Nordhurlanda*. Reykjavik: Islendingasagnautgafan, 1950, 4 vols.

Jung, Carl. *The Collected Works*. Princeton: Princeton University Press, 1960-1968, 18 vols.

Kaufmann, Friedrich. "Über den Schicksalsglauben der Germanen." *Zeitschrift fur deutsche Philologie*, 50 (1926), 361-408.

Kock, Ernst A., ed. *Den Norsk-Islandska Skaldediktningen*. Lund: Gleerup, 1946.

Larson, Gerlad J., ed. *Myth in Indo-European Antiquity*. Berkeley: University of California Press, 1974.

List, Guido von. *The Secret of the Runes*, tr. & ed. S. Flowers. Rochester, VT: Destiny, 1988.

Littleton, C. Scott. *The New Comparative Mythology: An Anthropological Assessment of the Theories of Georges Dumézil*. Berkeley: University of California Press, 1973.

Lother, Helmut. *Neugermanische Religion*. Gutersloh: Bertelsmann, 1937.

McNallen, Stephen A. *Rituals of Asatru: I Major Blots*. Breckenridge, TX: The Asatru Free Assembly, 1985.

_____. *Rituals of Asatru: II Seasonal Festivals*. Breckenridge, TX: The Asatru Free Assembly, 1985.

_____. *Rituals of Asatru: III Rites of Passage*. Breckenridge, TX: The Asatru Free Assembly, 1985.

Mannhardt, Wilhelm, *Wald- und Feldkulte*. Darmstadt: Wissenschaftliche Buchgesellschaft, 1963, 2 vols.

Martin, John S. *Ragnarok: An Investigation into Old Norse Concepts of the Fate of the Gods*. Assen: Van Gorcum, 1972.

Maurer, Konrad von. *Die Bekehrung des norwegischen Stammes zum Christentum*. Munich: Kaiser, 1855-56, 2 vols.

_____. "Über die Wasserweihe des germanischen Heidenthumes." *Abhandlungen der phil.-hist. Classe der königlich-bayrischen Akademie der Wissenschaften*, 15 (1881), pp. 173-253.

Mayer, Elard Hugo. *Germanische Mythologie*. Berlin: Mayer & Muller, 1891.

————. *Mythologie der Germanen*. Strassbourg: Trubner, 1903.

Motz, Lotte. "Withdrawal and Return: A Ritual Pattern in the Grettissaga." *Arkiv for Nordisk Filologi*, 88 (1973), pp. 91-110.

————. "Of Elves and Dwarves," *Arv* 29-30 (1973/74) pp. 93-127.

Much, Rudolf. *Die Germania des Tacitus*. Heidelberg: Winter, 1937.

Muller, Rolf. *Himmelskundliche Ortung auf nordisch-germanischem Boden*. Leipzig: Kabitzsch, 1936.

Mundal, Else. *Fylgemotiva in Norrøn Literatur*. Oslo: Universitetsforlaget, 1974.

Neckel, Gustav & Hans Kuhn, eds. *Edda, die Lieder der Codex Regius nebst verwandten Denkmalern*. Heidelberg: Winter, 1962.

Neff, Mary. "Germanic sacrifice: An analytical study using linguistic, archeological, and literary data." Diss.: University of Texas at Austin, 1980.

Neumann, Erich. *The Origins and History of Consciousness*, tr. R.F.C. Hull. New York: Pantheon, 1954.

————. *The Great Mother*, tr. Manheim. (Bollingen Series 47). Princeton: Princeton University Press, 1963.

Otto, Rudolf. *The Idea of the Holy*, tr. J. Harvey. New York: Oxford University Press, 1958.

Page, R.I. *An Introduction to English Runes*. London: Methuen, 1973.

Philippson, Ernst A. *Germanisches Heidentum bei den Angelsachsen*. Leipzig: Tauchnitz, 1929.

Polomé, Edgar C. "Some Comments on Voluspá Stanzas 17-18." In: *Old Norse Literature and Mythology: A Symposium*, ed. E.C. Polome. Austin: University of Texas Press, 1969.

————. "The Indo-European Component in Germanic Religion." In: *Myth and Law Among the Indo-Euro-*

peans: *Studies in Indo-European Comparative Mythology*, ed. J. Puhvel. Berkeley: University of California Press, 1970.

_____. "Approaches to Germanic Mythology." In: *Myth in Indo-European Antiquity*, ed. G. Larson. Berkeley: University of California Press, 1974.

Ranke, Kurt. "Ahnenglaube und Ahnenkult." *Reallexikon der germanischen Altertumskunde* 1:1 (1968), pp. 113-114.

Rusten, Rudolf. *Was tut not: Ein Führer durch die gesamte Literatur der Deutschbewegung*. Leipzig: Hedeler, 1914.

Saussaye, P.D. *The Religion of the Teutons*. New York: Ginn, 1902.

Saxo Grammaticus. *Saxonis Gesta Danorum*. Copenhagen: Levin & Munksgaard, 1931.

Schier, Kurt. *Sagaliteratur*. (= Sammlung Metzler 78). Stuttgart: Metzler, 1970.

Schneider, Hermann. *Germanische Heldensage*. Berlin: de Gruyter, 1934, 2 vols.

_____, ed. *Germanische Altertumskunde*. Munich: Beck, 1951.

Schröder, Franz Rolf. *Altgermanische Kulturprobleme*. Berlin: de Gruyter, 1929.

Schwarz, Ernst. *Germanische Stammeskunde*. Heidelberg: Winter, 1956.

See, Klaus von. *Deutsche Germanen-Ideologie: vom Humanismus bis zur Gegenwart*. Frankfurt/Main: Athenaum, 1970.

Slauson, Irv. *The Religion of Odin: A Handbook*. Red Wing, MN: The Asatru Free Church Committee, 1978.

Steblin-Kaminskij, M.I. *The Saga Mind*, tr. K.H. Ober. Odense: Odense Universitetsforlag, 1973.

Storm, Gustav. "Vore Forfædres Tro paa Sjaelevandring og deres Opkaldelesssytem." *Arkiv for Nordisk Filologi*,

9 (1893), 199-222.

Storms, G. *Anglo-Saxon Magic*. The Hague: Nijhoff, 1948.

Strom, Folke. *Den doendes Makt och Odin i Trädet*. Goteborg: Elaander, 1947.

_____. *Den egna Kraftens Man: En Studie i Forntida Irreligiositet*. Goteborg: Elander, 1948.

_____. *Diser, Nornor, Valkyrjor; Fruktbarheitskult och Sakralt Kungadome i Norden*. Stockholm: Almqvist & Wiksell, 1954.

_____. *Nidh, ergi, and Old Norse Moral Attitudes*. London: Viking Society, 1974.

Strömbäck, Dag. *Sejd*. Stockholm: Geber, 1935.

_____. "The Concept of the Soul in Nordic Tradition." *Arv* 31 (1975), 5-22.

Sturluson, Snorri. *The Prose Edda*, tr. A. Brodeur. New York: American Scandinavian Foundation, 1929.

_____. *The Prose Edda of Snorri Sturluson*, tr. Jean I. Young. Berkeley: University of California Press, 1964.

_____. *Heimskringla*, tr. Lee M. Hollander. Austin: University of Texas Press, 1964.

Strutynski, Udo. "Germanic Divinities in Weekday Names," *Journal of Indo-European Studies* 3 (1975), pp. 363-384.

Thorsson, Edred. *Futhark: A Handbook of Rune Magic*. York Beach, ME: Weiser, 1984.

_____. *Runelore: A Handbook of Esoteric Runology*. York Beach, ME: Weiser, 1987.

_____. *At the Well of Wyrd: A Handbook of Runic Divination*. York Beach, ME: Weiser, 1988.

Thümmel, Albert. *Der germanische Tempel*. Halle/Saale: Karras, 1909.

Turville-Petre, E.O.G. "A Note on the Landdisir." In: *Early English and Old Norse Studies*, A. Brown, ed. London: Methuen, 1963.

_____. *Myth and Religion of the North*. New York: Holt,

Rinehart & Winston, 1964.

Vries, Jan de. *Altgermanische Religionsgeschichte*. Berlin: de Gruyter, 1937, 2 vols.

_____. "Der Mythos von Baldrs Tod." *Arkiv for Nordisk Filologi* 70 (1955), pp. 41-60.

_____. *Altgermanische Religionsgeschichte*. Berlin: de Gruyter, 1956/57, 2 vols.

_____. *Altnordisches etymologisches Worterbuch*. Leiden: Brill, 1961.

_____. *Altnordische Literaturgeschichte*. Berlin: de Gruyter, 1964, 2 vols.

Watkins, Calvert. "Language of Gods and Language of Men: Remarks on Some Indo-European Metalinguistic Traditions" In: *Myth and Law among the Indo-Europeans*, ed. J. Puhvel. Berkeley: University of California Press, 1970, pp. 1-17.

Wenskus, Reinhard. *Stammesbildung und Verfassung: Das Werden der frühmittelalterlichen gentes*. Cologne: Bohlau, 1961.

Wesche, Heinrich. *Der althochdeutsche Wortschatz im Gebeite des Zaubers und der Weissagung*. Halle/Saale: Niemeyer, 1940.

Williams, Mary. *Social Scandinavia in the Viking Age*. New York: Macmillan, 1930.

STAY IN TOUCH

On the following pages you will find listed, with their current prices, some of the books and tapes now available on related subjects. Your book dealer stocks most of these, and will stock new titles in the Llewellyn series as they become available. We urge your patronage.

However, to obtain our full catalog, to keep informed of new titles as they are released and to benefit from informative articles and helpful news, you are invited to write for our bi-monthly news magazine/catalog. A sample copy is free, and it will continue coming to you at no cost as long as you are an active mail customer. Or you may keep it coming for a full year with a donation of just $5.00 in U.S.A. and Canada ($20.00 overseas, first class mail). Many bookstores also have *The Llewellyn New Times* available to their customers. Ask for it.

Stay in touch! In *The Llewellyn New Times'* pages you will find news and reviews of new books, tapes and services, announcements of meetings and seminars, articles helpful to our readers, news of authors, advertising of products and services, special money-making opportunities, and much more.

The Llewellyn New Times
P.O. Box 64383-Dept. 777, St. Paul, MN 55164-0383, U.S.A.

• • •

TO ORDER BOOKS AND TAPES

If your book dealer does not have the books and tapes described on the following pages readily available, you may order them directly from the publisher by sending full price in U.S. funds, plus $1.50 for postage and handling for orders *under* $10.00; $3.00 for orders *over* $10.00. There are no postage and handling charges for orders over $50.00. UPS Delivery: We ship UPS whenever possible. Delivery guaranteed. Provide your street address as UPS does not deliver to P.O. Boxes. UPS to Canada requires a $50.00 minimum order. Allow 4-6 weeks for delivery. Orders outside the U.S.A. and Canada: Airmail—add retail price of book; add $5.00 for each non-book item (tapes, etc.); add $1.00 per item for surface mail.

FOR GROUP STUDY AND PURCHASE

Because there is a great deal of interest in group discussion and study of the subject matter of this book, we feel that we should encourage the adoption and use of this particular book by such groups by offering a special "quantity" price to group leaders or "agents."

Our Special Quantity Price for a minimum order of five copies of *The Book of Troth* is $29.85 cash-with-order. This price includes postage and handling within the United States. Minnesota residents must add 6.5% sales tax. For additional quantities, please order in multiples of five. For Canadian and foreign orders, add postage and handling charges as above. Credit card (VISA, Master Card, American Express) orders are accepted. Charge card orders only may be phoned free ($15.00 minimum order) within the U.S.A. or Canada by dialing 1-800-THE-MOON. Customer service calls dial 1-612-291-1970. Mail Orders to:

LLEWELLYN PUBLICATIONS
P.O. Box 64383-Dept. 777 / St. Paul, MN 55164-0383, U.S.A.

THE RITES OF ODIN
by Ed Fitch

The ancient Northern Europeans knew a rough magic drawn from the grandeur of vast mountains and deep forests, of rolling oceans and thundering storms. Their rites and beliefs sustained the Vikings, accompanying them to the New World and to the Steppes of Central Asia. Now, for the first time, this magic system is brought compellingly into the present by author Ed Fitch.

This is a complete source volume on Odinism. It stresses the ancient values as well as the magic and myth of this way of life. The author researched his material in Scandinavia and Germany, and drew from anthropological and historical sources in Eastern and Central Europe.

A full cycle of ritual is provided, with rites of passage, magical spells, divination techniques, and three sets of seasonal rituals: solitary, group and family. *The Rites of Odin* also contain extensive "how-to" sections on planning and conducting Odinist ceremonies, including preparation of ceremonial implements and the setting up of ritual areas. Each section is designed to stand alone for easier reading and for quick reference. A bibliography is provided for those who wish to pursue the historical and anthropological roots of Odinism further.

0-87542-224-1, 360 pgs., 6 x 9, illus., softcover   **$12.95**

FIRE & ICE
Magical Teachings of Germany's Greatest Secret Occult Order
by S. Edred Flowers

The hidden beliefs and practices of German occultism have long held a strong fascination for the poet as well as the historian. The greatest of the modern German secret lodges—the Fraternitas Saturni—revealed neither its membership, its beliefs, nor its rites. Through a chance occurrence, the inner documents of this order were recently published in Germany. *Fire & Ice* is the first comprehensive study of these documents, and the inner workings of the FS which they reveal, to be published in any language.

This book relates the fascinating histories of the founders and leaders of the Fraternitas Saturni. You will witness the development of its magical beliefs and practices, its banishment by the Nazi government, and its many postwar dissensions and conflicts. The Saturnian path of initiation will be revealed in full detail, and the magical formulas which are included can be used for your own self-development as well as for more practical and concrete goals.

Fire & Ice throws a unique light on one of the world's darkest and most mysterious philosophical corners. No matter what your magical system may be, you will learn much from the adherents of Fire & Ice!

0-87542-776-6, 240 pgs., 5-1/4 x 8, illus., softcover   **$9.95**

RUNE MIGHT: Secret Practices of the German Rune Magicians
by Edred Thorsson

Rune Might reveals, for the first time in the English language, the long-hidden secrets of the German rune magicians who practiced their arts in the beginning of this century. By studying the contents of *Rune Might* and working with the exercises, the reader will be introduced to a fascinating world of personalities and the sometimes sinister dark corners of runic history. Beyond this, the reader will be able to experience the direct power of the runes as experienced by the early German rune magicians.

Rune Might takes the best and most powerful of the runic techniques developed in that early phase of the runic revival and offers them as a coherent set of exercises. Experience rune yoga, rune dance, runic hand gestures (mudras), rune singing (mantras), group rites with runes, runic healing, runic geomancy, and two of the most powerful runic methods of engaging transpersonal powers—the Ritual of the Ninth Night and the Ritual of the Grail Cup.

The exercises represent bold new methods of drawing magical power into your life—regardless of the magical tradition or system with which you normally work. No other system does this in quite the direct and clearly defined ways that rune exercises do.

0-87542-778-2, 192 pgs., 5¼ × 8, illustrated **$7.95**

THE TRUTH ABOUT TEUTONIC MAGICK
by Edred Thorsson

You may have heard about Teutonic magick, but what is it really? In this illuminating booklet you will learn that this largely ignored and often misunderstood system of magickal practice has actually been a major influence on what is known as the Western Occult Tradition.

In *The Truth about Teutonic Magick*, you will begin to discover some of the rich lore and myths of this powerful ancient tradition:

- the cosmic mystery of the runes—a magickal map of human consciousness.
- *seidhr*—the practice of traveling to other dimensions of reality.
- rituals of the troth—Hallowing, Blessing, Drinking, and more.
- sacred cycle of the year—Disting, Walburga, Yule, etc.
- the gods and goddesses of the troth—Woden, Freya, Thor, and others.
- the divine realms and the World-Tree, Yggdrasil.

The Teutonic tradition is as rich and varied as the Hermetic or Kabbalistic systems, and it is attracting increasing interest among students of High Magick.

0-87542-779-0, 32 pgs., 5½ × 8½, illus. **$2.00**

RUNE MAGIC
by Donald Tyson

Drawing upon historical records, poetic fragments, and the informed study of scholars, *Rune Magic* resurrects the ancient techniques of this tactile form of magic, and integrates those methods with modern occultism, so that anyone can use the runes in a personal magical system. For the first time, every known and conjectured meaning of all 33 known runes, including the 24 runes known as *futhark*, is available in one volume. In addition, *Rune Magic* covers the use of runes in divination, astral traveling, skrying, and on amulets and talismans. A complete rune ritual is also provided, and 24 rune words are outlined. Gods and Goddesses of the runes are discussed, with illustrations from the National Museum of Sweden.

0-87542-826-6, 224 pgs., 6 × 9, illus., softcover   **$9.95**

RUNE MAGIC CARDS
created by Donald Tyson

Llewellyn Publications presents, for the first time ever, *Rune Magic Cards* created by Donald Tyson. This unique divinatory deck consists of 24 strikingly designed cards, boldly portraying a Germanic *futhark* Rune on each card. Robin Wood has illuminated each Rune Card with graphic illustrations done in the ancient Norse tradition. Included on each card are the old English name, its meaning, the phonetic value of the Rune, and its number in Roman numerals. Included with this deck is a complete instruction booklet, which includes magical workings, sample spreads and a wealth of information culled from years of study.

0-87542-827-4, 24 cards, booklet   **$12.95**

THE POWER OF THE RUNES
by Donald Tyson

This kit contains *Rune Magic*, Tyson's highly acclaimed guide to effective runework. In this book he clears away misconceptions surrounding this magical alphabet of the Northern Europeans, provides information on the Gods and Goddesses of the runes, and gives the meanings and uses of all 33 extant runes. The reader will be involved with practical runic rituals and advice on talisman, amulet and sigil use.

The Power of the Runes also includes the *Rune Magic Deck*. This set of 24 large cards illustrates each of the Futhark runes in a stunning 2-color format. This is the first deck ever published, which makes it not only unique, but truly historical!

We have also included a set of wooden rune dice, with their own cloth bag, in this kit. These four dice, each ¾" square, were designed by Donald Tyson himself. The user casts them down, then interprets their meanings as they appear before him or her. With the 24 Futhark runes graphically etched on their sides, these dice let the user perform an accurate reading in mere seconds.

0-87542-828-2, 224-page book, 24-card deck, 4 dice, bag   **$24.95**

A PRACTICAL GUIDE TO THE RUNES:
Their Uses in Divination and Magick
by Lisa Peschel

At last the world has a book on the Nordic runes that is written in straightforward and clear language. Each of the 25 runes is elucidated through no-nonsense descriptions and clean graphics. A rune's altered meaning in relation to other runes and its reversed position is also included.The construction of runes and accessories covers such factors as the type of wood to be used, the size of the runes, and the coloration, carving and charging of the runes.With this book the runes can be used in magick to effect desired results. Talismans carved with runescripts or bindrunes allow you to carry your magick in a tangible form, providing foci for your will. Four rune layouts complete with diagrams are presented with examples of specific questions to ask when consulting the runes. Rather than simple fortunetelling devices, the runes are oracular, empowered with the forces of Nature. They present information for you to make choices in your life.

0-87542-593-3, 192 pgs., mass market, illus. $3.95

NORTHERN MAGIC: Mysteries of the Norse, Germans & English
by Edred Thorsson

This in-depth primer of the magic of the Northern Way introduces the major concepts and practices of Gothic or Germanic magic. English, German, Dutch, Icelandic, Danish, Norwegian, and Swedish peoples are all directly descended from this ancient Germanic cultural stock. According to author Edred Thorsson, if you are interested in living a holistic life with unity of body-mind-spirit, a key to knowing your spiritual heritage is found in the heritage of your body—in the natural features which you have inherited from your distant ancestors. Most readers of this book already "speak the language" of the Teutonic tradition.

Northern Magic contains material that has never before been discussed in a practical way. This book outlines the ways of Northern magic and the character of the Northern magician. It explores the theories of traditional Northern psychology (or the lore of the soul) in some depth, as well as the religious tradition of the Troth and the whole Germanic theology. The r remaining chapters make up a series of "mini-grimoires" on four basic magical techniques in the Northern way: Younger Futhark, rune magic, Icelandic galdor staves, Pennsylvania Dutch hex signs, and *seith* (or shamanism).

This is an excellent overview of the Teutonic Tradition that will interest neophytes as well as long-time travelers, along the Northern Way.

0-87542-782-0, 320 pgs., mass market, illus. $4.95